Publication Details
45 Days

Published by Parris Publishing

Cover picture adapted from a photograph taken from Manus Alert.

45 DAYS

Dedicated to Man Man, who has recently moved from detention on
Manus Island, Papua New Guinea to Atlanta, Georgia in the USA
and to all those brave heroes who
are still held illegally on Manus Island.

Each man incarcerated on Manus is a unique human being
who simply boarded a boat and sailed towards Australia
in search of freedom.

FOREWORD

Those of you who have read Jill's previous book about Man Man and their unlikely friendship, will be relieved to hear he has been accepted for resettlement in the United States. You will laugh and cry with him on his journey through the migration process, and wonder with him what the future holds in this new home. This sequel to "Man Man - Making meaning on Manus" is a serious book that shouts out serious truths.

Firstly, indefinite detention in a prison with no checks and balances destroys the human soul. Not all at once, but by slow stages.

Secondly, the Australian government uses arbitrary cruelty, not only to deter people smugglers, but to win votes as part of a strategy which uses racism to divide the nation. To show how tough they are, and how far they are prepared to go to defend us.

Lastly, it is a book about human resilience. How the men detained on Manus have grown their own community of support in the face of relentless cruelty and destabilisation. How hard it is for Man Man to come to terms with his survivor guilt, to build a future without forgetting the past. He is one in a long series who have had to face this transition – survivors of the trenches in WWI, survivors of Auschwitz in WWII, but one of those, like Mandela, who seem to come out not only with their humanity intact, but enriched.

This is an important book, because books that record man's inhumanity to man are always important. Books that record and celebrate survival are important.

Hayshiv.
(David Parris)

My name is Man Man and I give Jill Parris permission to use all my pictures and messages in this book.

INTRODUCTION

HISTORY

My intention with this book is twofold. Firstly to focus our attention on the day to day struggle of the brave heroes incarcerated on Manus Island and secondly to share Man's emotional and physical journey from Manus to the USA.

This diary covers only 45 days in the lives of the Manus detainees from 10 December 2017 to 23 January 2018. Focusing on this time has been exhausting and I can simply not comprehend what life has been like for those who have been banished for well over four years. The first men to be incarcerated in the reopened Manus centre have now been in detention for just short of 5 years.

Manus Island Regional Processing Centre Lombrum was opened on 21 November 2012. The men held on Manus came largely from the Middle East including countries such as Afghanistan, Iraq and Pakistan. On 26 April 2016, the Supreme Court of Papua New Guinea found that the Centre breached the PNG constitution's right to personal liberty, and was thus illegal. Lombrum was officially closed on October 31, 2017. In a report updated by Mary Anne Kenny of Murdoch University on the 23rd of November 2017 there were still about 420 in this centre. There are now no men left at Lombrum.

This is a small, sanitised, part of their story.

MY VIEW OF THE PRESENT DRIVERS OF THE LIBERAL GOVERNMENT

I am not an independent observer but try to keep my personal political views out of my advocacy.
Based on "news headlines" our leaders, concerned about "losing the next election" are presently focused on:
- devoting prodigious resources to building a Homeland security department based on the "American model"
- detaining all asylum seekers in on- and offshore detention for extended periods of time
- immediately processing protection applications for 7,500 asylum seekers not previously assessed.

> **Scott Morrison tried to delay asylum seekers' permanent protection visas, documents reveal**
> Scott Morrison agreed his department should intervene in ASIO security checks to try to prevent asylum seekers from being granted permanent protection visas, according to cabinet documents obtained by the ABC.
> In late 2013, the then-immigration minister was rushing through changes that would prevent any asylum seekers who arrived by boat from ever being granted permanent protection in Australia.
> see http://www.abc.net.au/news/2018-01-30/scott-morrison-tried-to-delay-asylum-seekers-visas/ 9353350

THE DIARY FORMAT

I have used a diary format to bring together Manus news under a banner headline. The inside view of the men trapped in Manus detention is extracted from "Manus Alert" a blog writen by the detainees to share their plight with the world, The time between Man being told he would leave Manus and his departure for the USA draws on the day to day communication between him and me on Facebook Messenger.

It would have been easier to simply write a chapter on each of these but I hope the use of a diary highlights the excruciating slow processes of every day life in detention.

Australia's Manus Island detention camp: a time-line

Extracted from an article written in Le Courrier Austtalien on 24th November 2017

2016: The Papua New Guinea Supreme Court says the Manus Island centre violates the constitution and must be closed.

Canberra complies, but insists the detainees must be moved to other camps or resettled in third countries.

In September, 24 men leave Manus for the United States under a resettlement deal.

'Humanitarian emergency'

October 11, 2017: Australia offers to move Manus detainees to family camps on Nauru. Few accept.

October 31: Canberra declares the Manus camp closed and cuts off power, water and food supplies. Some 600 detainees refuse to leave, fearing for their safety in the PNG-run transit camps.

November 2: The UN calls the situation a "humanitarian emergency".

November 5: Australian Prime Minister Malcolm Turnbull brushes aside a renewed offer from New Zealand to resettle 150 of the men at Manus, saying their resettlement in the US remains the priority.

November 9: PNG authorities threaten to use force, and enter the camp in the following days to destroy shelters and water containers to force departures.

On November 23, PNG police raid the camp, destroying belongings and forcing around 50 refugees onto buses bound for transit centres.

Some 350 men remain.

An extract from A letter from Manus Island by Behrouz Boochani (A detainee and journalist on Man.

From the standpoint of someone operating at the core of the resistance for this long period of time – that is, the whole three-week period – and privy to everything that was happening inside the prison and the details of the resistance, I think the only thing that helped us persevere for the long stretch of time was our dedication to principles of humanity and human values.

In the community meetings we held every day at 5pm, we stayed true to the principles of love, friendship and brotherhood. (Boochani is a journealist who is detained on Manus)

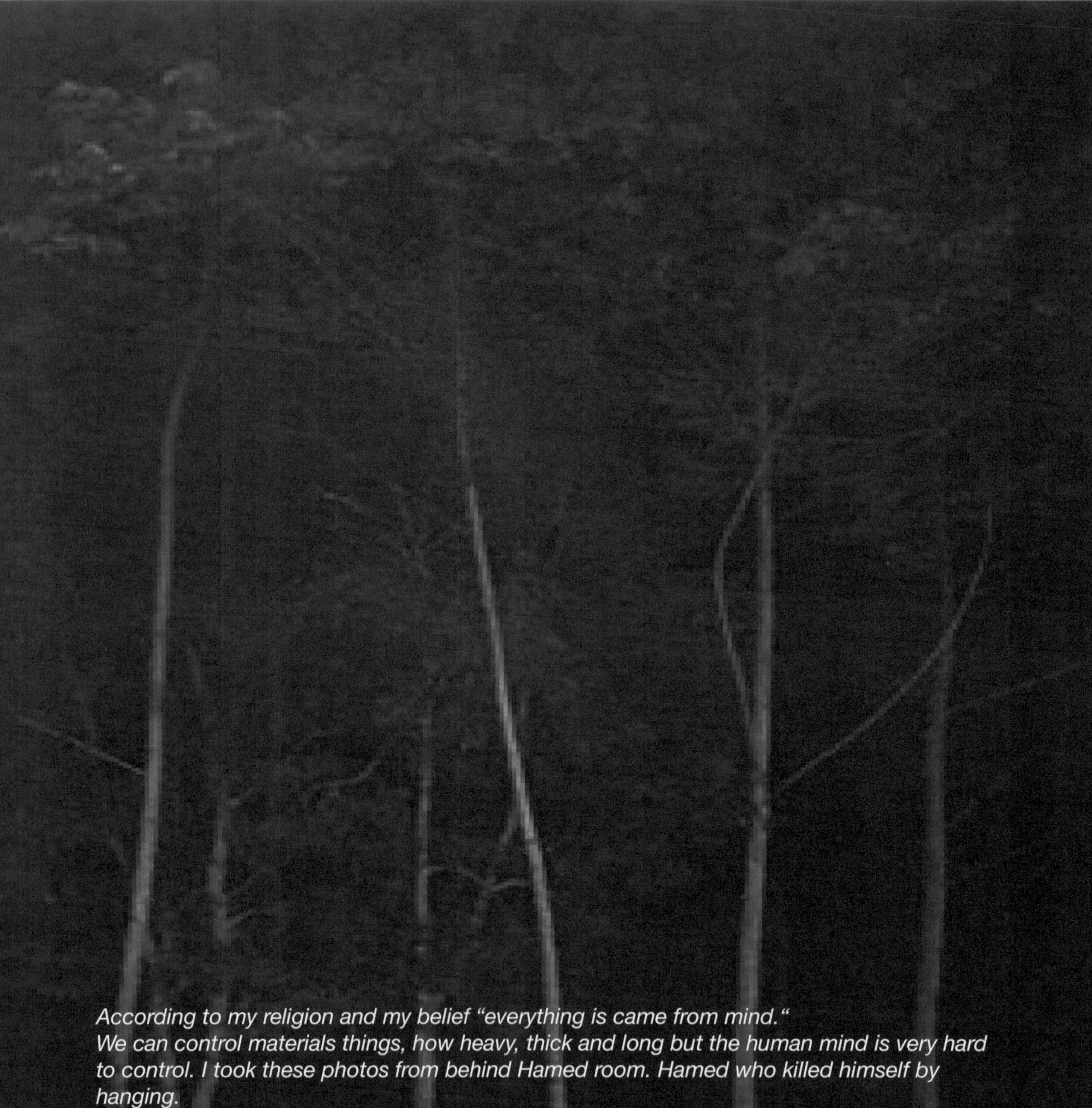

According to my religion and my belief "everything is came from mind."
We can control materials things, how heavy, thick and long but the human mind is very hard
to control. I took these photos from behind Hamed room. Hamed who killed himself by
hanging.

MANUS ALERT MAN ON MESSENGER

VOICES FROM MANUS:
We are not going to give up until we get our freedom it's day 125th peaceful protest Easter Lorengu prison camp.

All human beings are born free and equal in dignity and rights. Give us our rights.

We believe life is not forever, but you already took 1592 days from our lifes. This is not enough for you? No More Hope.

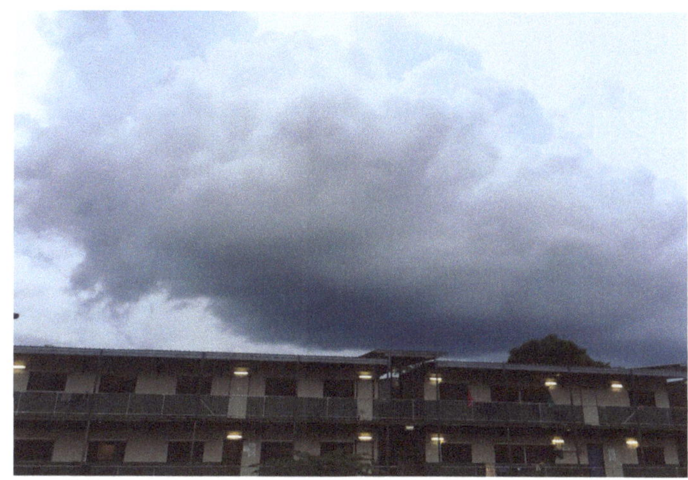

MAN:
We are more hopeless in here.
I'm sure that we will be in here too long or forever. That's why I said that no return way Island. It's ok aunty. I know that it is not your decision.

JILL: I am sorry Man.

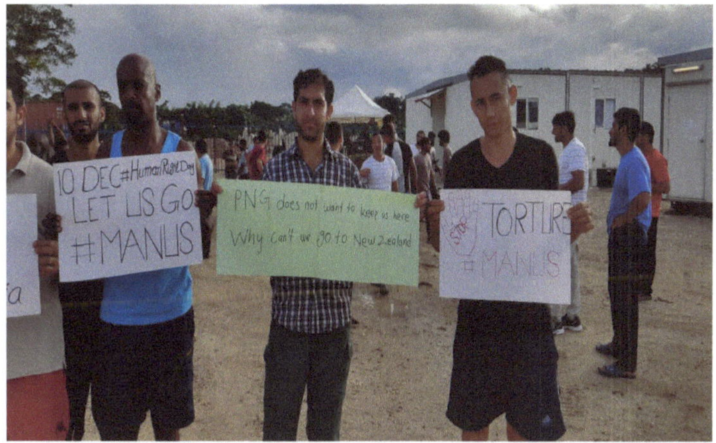

It is excruciating to sit with the pain. Some men have been on Manus for almost five years. Many have been away from family and home countries much longer. All say they cannot return. Recently many men have refused to leave Lombrum camp. Man remained as part of this silent resistance for three weeks. Every day was fraught but Man gained strength through solidarity. He did not speak of his hunger or thirst and only left when he became concerned for his survival. I was pleased he left. In Lombrum Man, always stoic, grew hopeless. Pictures of a forest outside his window capture his despair. He said "here is where my friend Hamed hung himself".

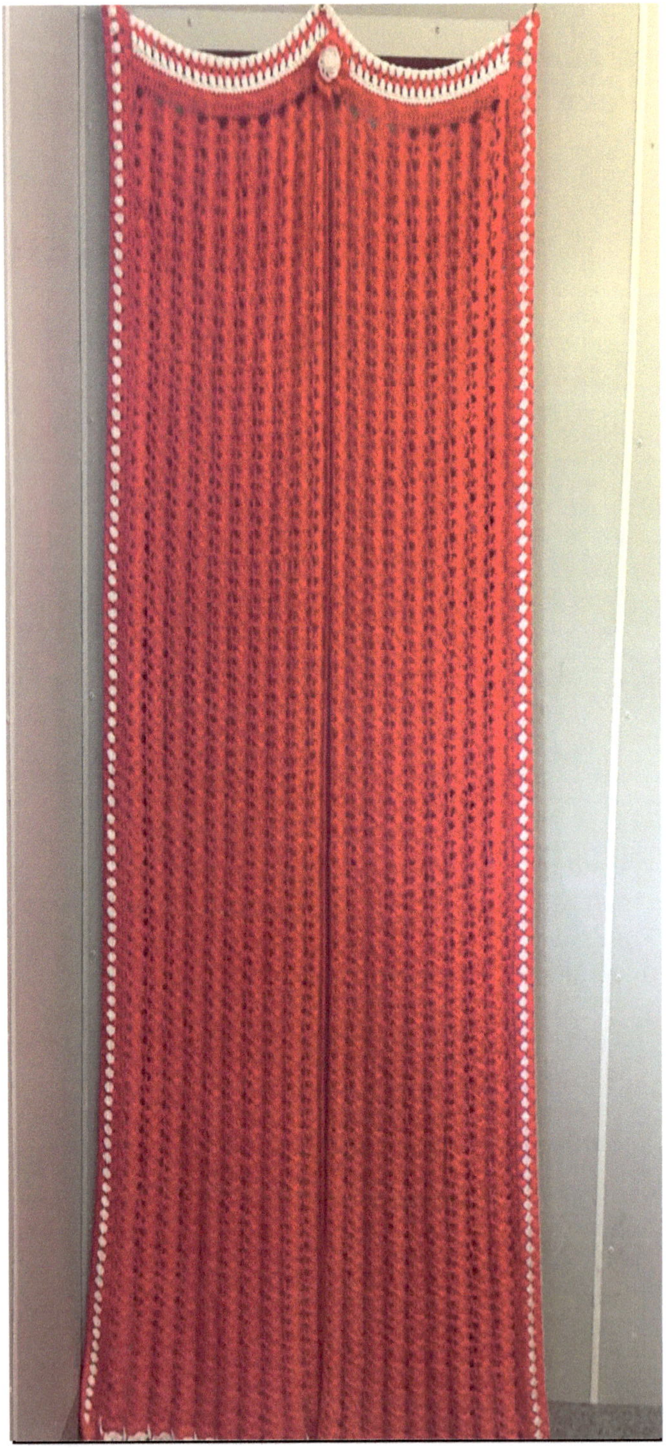

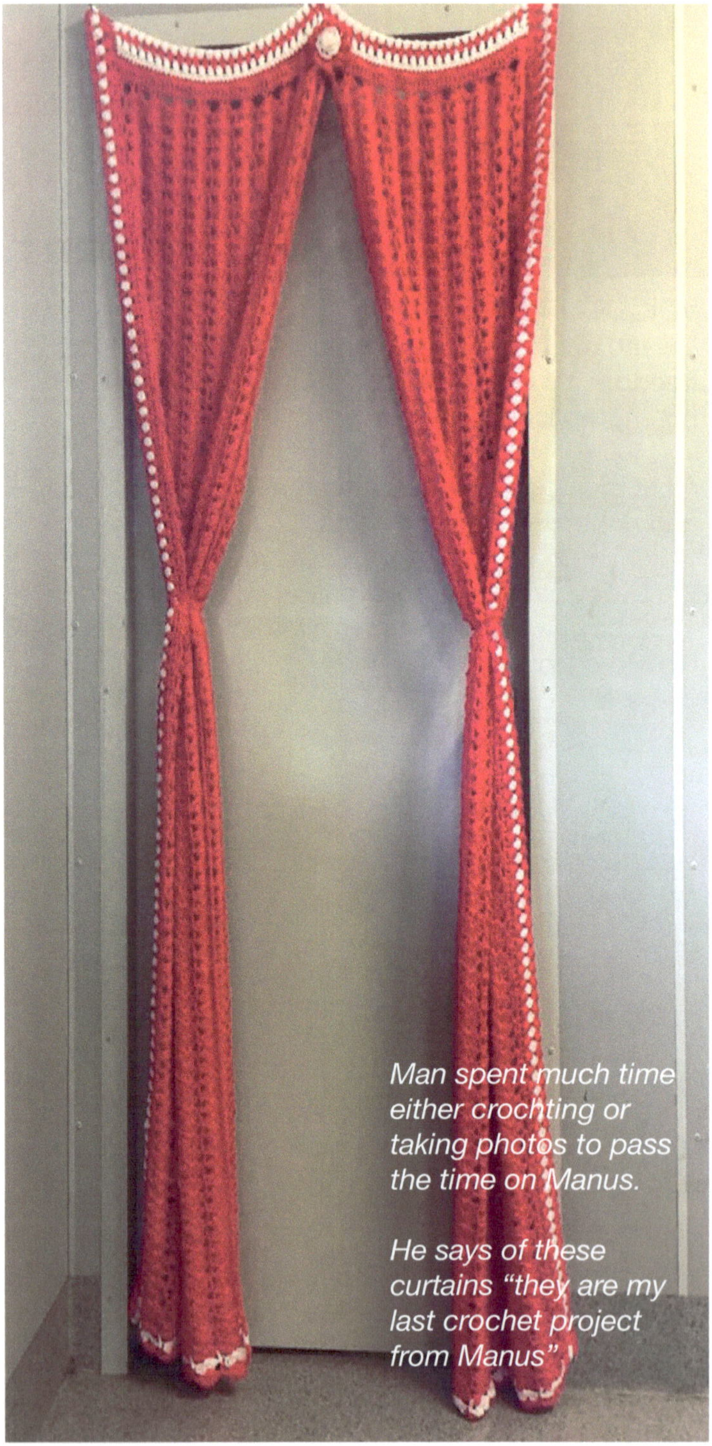

Man spent much time
either crochting or
taking photos to pass
the time on Manus.

He says of these
curtains "they are my
last crochet project
from Manus"

"The evidence is overwhelming. Indefinite detention is causing serious damage to health and wellbeing. There is evidence that many Manus patients become more ill and acquire addictions and additional medical problems because of the treatment." Jane Irene Koegh

MANUS ALERT   MAN ON MESSENGER

West Haus peaceful protest 130.

NZ wants to give us freedom
We are happy to live in NZ
PNG doesn't want to keep us here
Why can't we go to NZ?

Slaves of Australia.

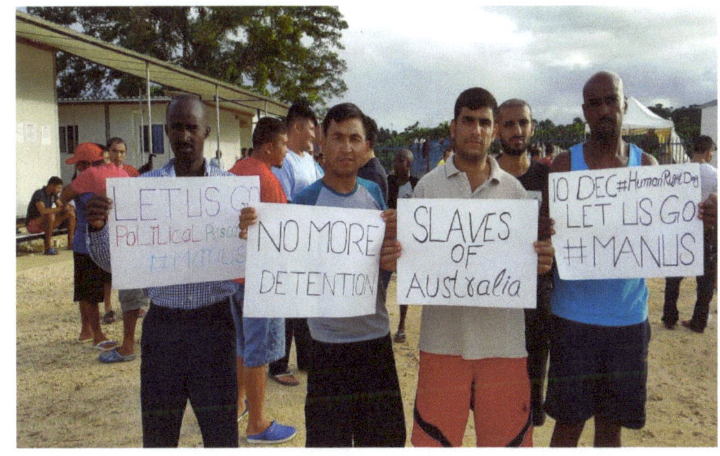

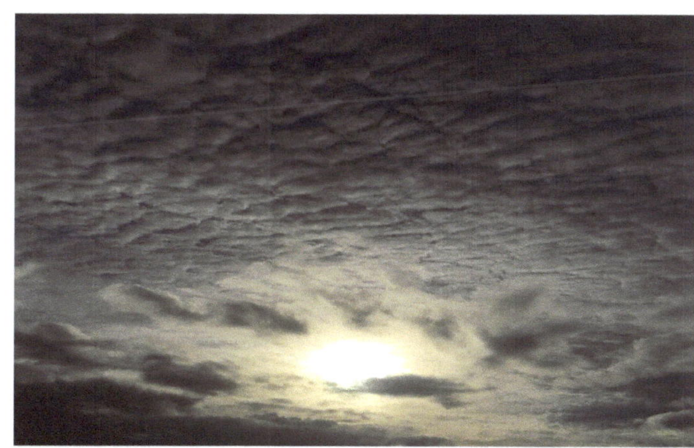

JILL: Enjoy today Man. It may be your last on Manus.

MAN:
I'll be busy with packing today. I think the meeting is about a flight to Pom (Port Moresby) form Manus, this morning I met with an Australian man who said that it's for USA and for paper words then flight to USA.

What a relief that Man will finally be leaving. Resilient for so long and yet I have often wondered how useful his self-protective Buddhist approach is. Man has managed to be on Manus almost without being part of the detention population. He has often seen himself as doing things to support others rather than as one of them. He has always been his own man, not bound by some of the constraints of others. He has spoken freely with guards and support workers even when warned against this.

Now as I celebrate Man's reprieve I feel guilty and if I focus on the suffering of those left behind I am heartbroken. I want to flee the devastation of offshore detention with Man.

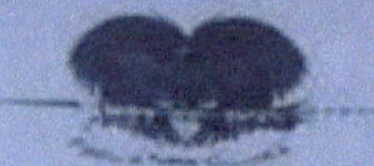

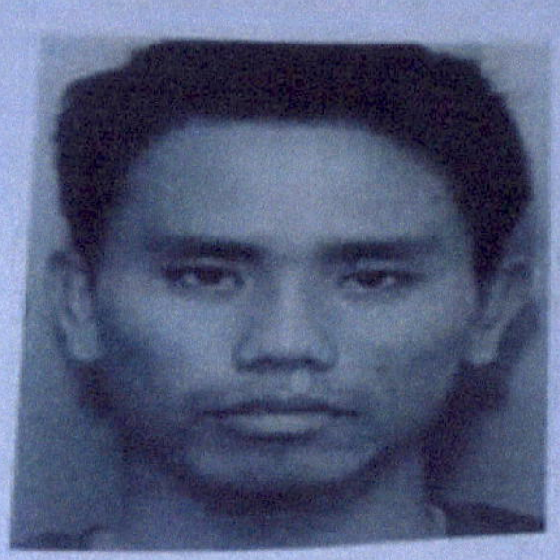

STATEMENT OF IDENTITY

I, Dennis Badi, am an officer for the purposes of the Migration Act 1978 I declare that the bearer of this document and the person whose image appears in the attached photograph is known to the PNG Immigration Citizenship Service Authority as:

Name: Aung Saw LIM
Citizenship: MYANMAR
Language: BURMESE
DOB: 23/09/1992
Boat ID: ROD062

This Statement of Identity is for the purposes for travel and identification to open a bank account in PNG.

Dennis Badi
Operations Manager
Manus Regional Processing Centre (MRPC)
Refugee Division | Regional Processing Centres Branch | Lombrum
PNG Immigration and Citizenship Service Authority
08 December 2017

JILL: The first time you have been called by name in over 4 years. What would you like me to call you.
MAN: Whatever.
I like Man Man or Lim.
Lim is my Dad race
Man Man is just my family called me.

<table>
<tr><td>

</td><td>

QUOTE FROM A MANUSIAN ISLANDER:
"So many of us are horrified. This is so unacceptable. I am so lost for words. The result of Australia's Offshore Processing. It's not working Australia. It's causing harm to human lives. And it has caused deaths".

</td></tr>
</table>

MANUS ALERT

MAN ON MESSENGER

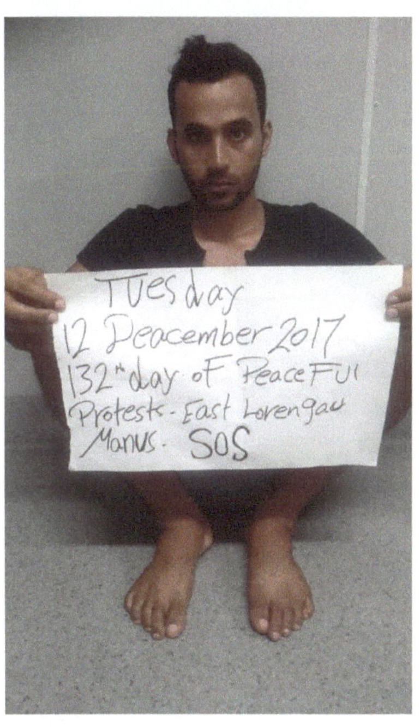

East Lorengau Transit centre has so little space, there are not even corridors for men to protest. Silent in-room protest

Tuesday
12 December 2017
132nd day of Peaceful Protests.

Today heavy rain here. Rain clothes & umbrellas destroyed in attack on us in Lombrum detention. We could not go outside today.

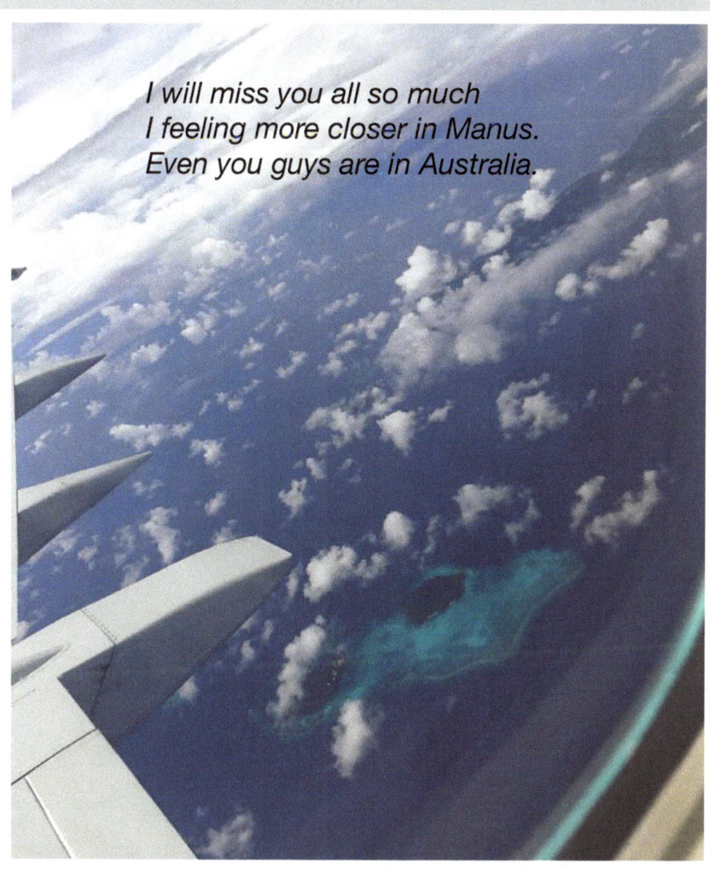

I got to know Man through his photography and have enjoyed a mutual friendship built on sharing pictures, but there have been dark times. In the last couple of days Man has begun to be more open emotionally. He is excited about leaving, concerned about going to the USA, anxious about the departure process and overwhelmingly scared for the people he is leaving behind. Knowing that Man is leaving Manus has freed me to accept my enormous fear that many Manus men may perish.

58 Manus men have appointments with the US Resettlement Support Centre in Port Moresby.
They leave for Port Moresby on Monday 11/12/17 and on Wednesday 13/12/17.

Men from three countries were offered appointments: Myanmar (28), Afghanistan (20) &
Pakistan (10).

No Sudanese, Iranian, Sri Lankan, Somalian, Syrian, Lebanese or Iraqi men were offered
appointments with the US Resettlement Support Centre in Port Moresby.

23 sick men were given notices. Only 3 boarded the bus. 20 refused because the notices
were wrong, they are still sick. They are still in Port Moresby

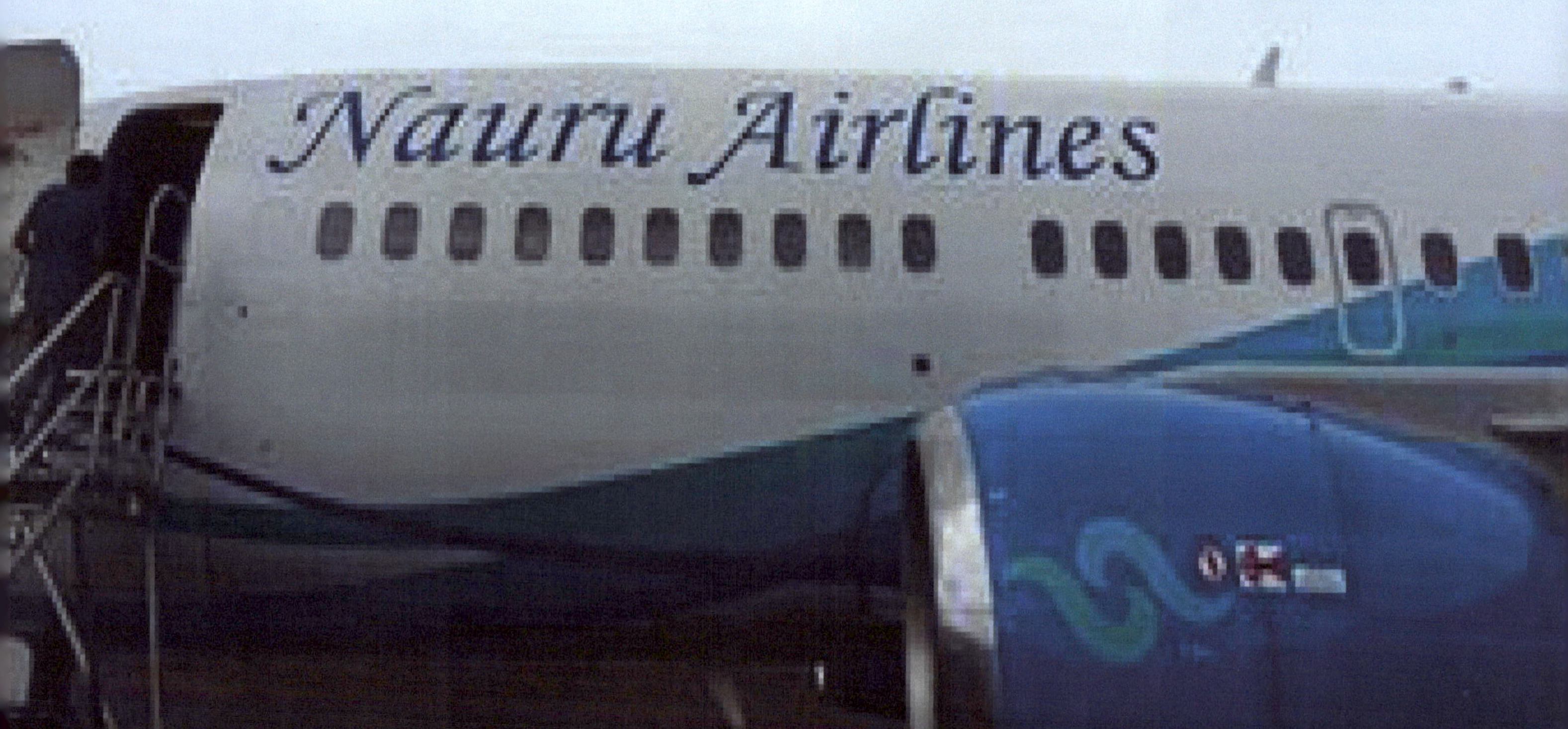

<table>
<tr><td>

13

DEC

2017

</td><td>

Mr Turnbull said "There are a number of people-smuggling boats that have been intercepted by our Operation Sovereign Borders. He also said that "ruthless" people smugglers had been "very busily marketing and promoting New Zealand as a destination recently".

</td></tr>
</table>

MANUS ALERT

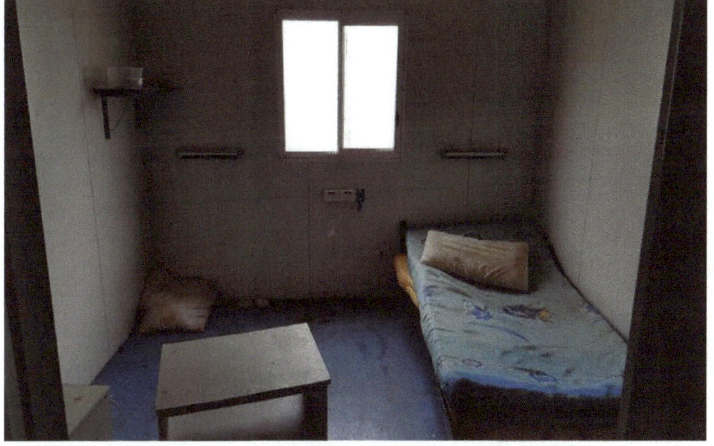

Peter Dutton lied when he said the new accommodation facilities where ready on Manus & were five star. This is the new accommodation delivered to west camp yesterday Monday.

Amir Taghinia addresses Amnesty International, Canada.
After 4+ years detention on Manus Is. Amir is now in Canada & continues to raise awareness of Australia's atrocities on Manus & Nauru.

MAN ON MESSENGER

MAN: Just I felt sad feeling on my way.
JILL: Because you have got used to Manus?
MAN: No.
I left to Abu and some friends.
I would like to leave with them from Manus.
JILL: Of course it is hard to leave them there.
MAN: Then I saw two Irani men who are double negative. Serco handcuffed to them. Made me so sad. Too sad. The flight is charter flight Nauru airline. They are going to Pom with the men going from Manus medical treatment.
But Serco and Wilson staff are working in the plane. It's Australian government who influence the PNG government because no PNG immigration officer checked us even in Port Morsby airport.
There were no PNG immigration or police only Serco and Wilson. The Australian government says that the responsibility lies with the PNG government.
Aunty I am so worried about my friend Abu.

("double negative" assessment of refugee status means people are not seen as genuine asylum seekers and can face forced deportation.)

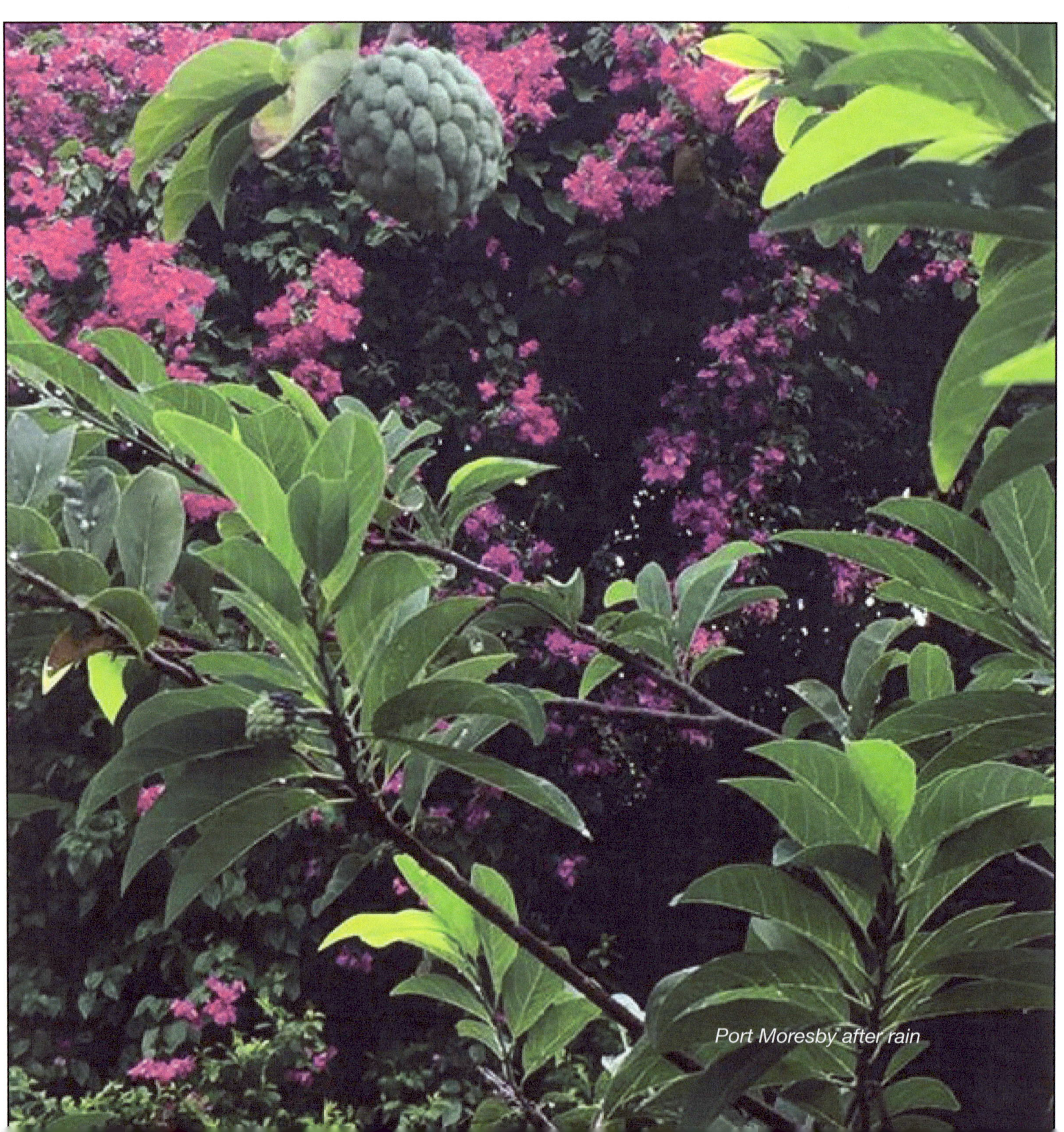
Port Moresby after rain

"**Second cohort of Nauru and Manus refugees to be resettled in US. The majority of refugees accepted for resettlement in the current group are from Pakistan, Afghanistan, and stateless Rohingyans from Myanmar and Bangladesh.**" The Guardian

MANUS ALERT

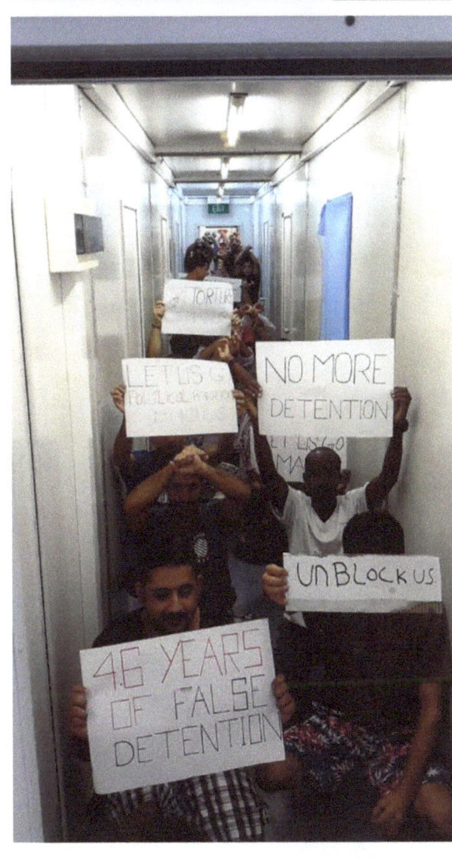

4.6 years of false detention
Unblock us
No more detention
Stop torture
Manus
Let us go #Manus.

134th day of peaceful protests
Waste West Haus

(West Hous is a new and incomplete detention centre)

MAN ON MESSENGER

MAN: Aunt I'm very sad for Middle Eastern people They are thinking of their future and feeling very hopeless. It's the same for positive men because of Trump's travel ban policy.

JILL: I know it is awful. It feels like the world's anger never ends.

MAN: I'm just sad and sigh for them.
I came from an Islamphobic country but I lived with them for above four years that's why I knew about them. They are very kind people and friendly and easy believers. That's why Western world could make conflicts in Middle East countries.

JILL: Man it is wonderful that you are able to love and I have such respect for you all wherever you come from.

MAN: I could imagine that why Western world could be conflict in there because they are a bit lazy and a bit stupid and not united.

JILL: Oh Man it's not all of any race but you have lost faith. I believe any man is capable of good or evil, and I know there are good people in the USA.

MAN: I love Middle Eastern people.

JILL: I try to love all people but don't always get it right.

MAN: When I lived in Myanmar I feared Middle Eastern people because of rumors but we have lived together for over four years. I love them and am upset.

I smile at Man's simple reminder of the growing prejudice and racism in Australia. Xenophobia has been part of Australia since the "white" man first landed here. This government builds and thrives on it.

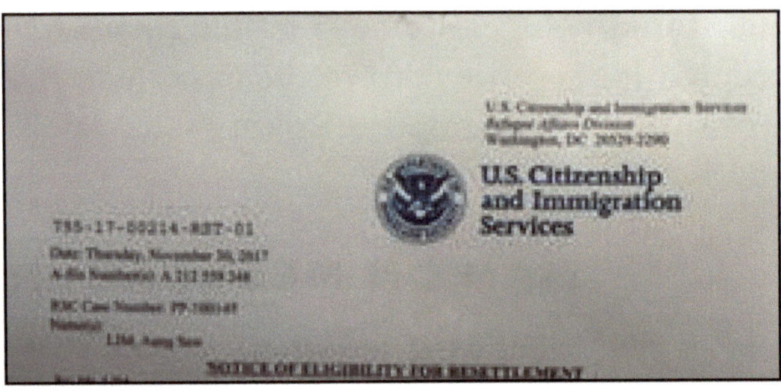

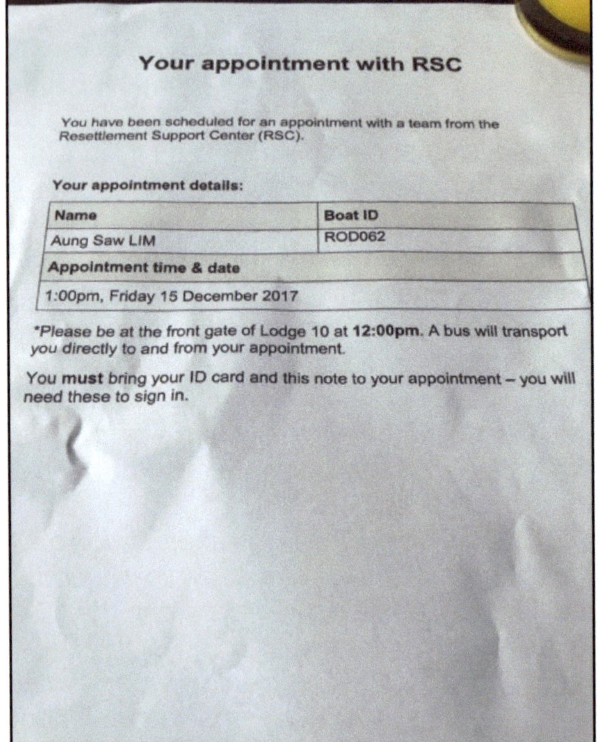

Your appointment with RSC

You have been scheduled for an appointment with a team from the Resettlement Support Center (RSC).

Your appointment details:

Name	Boat ID
Aung Saw LIM	ROD062

Appointment time & date	
1:00pm, Friday 15 December 2017	

*Please be at the front gate of Lodge 10 at **12:00pm**. A bus will transport you directly to and from your appointment.

You **must** bring your ID card and this note to your appointment — you will need these to sign in.

MAN: This document is from US gov . It meant approved me to go USA
So next two or three weeks we can fly to USA

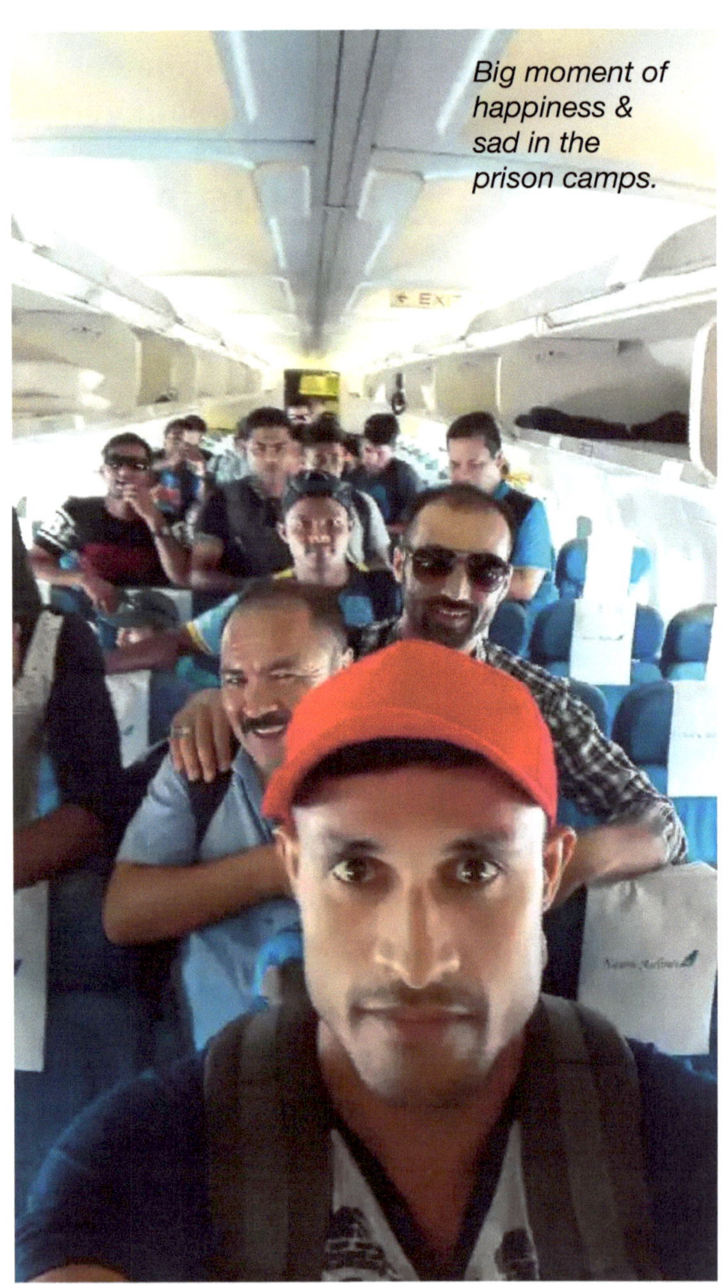

Health professionals in Darwin call for action for refugees "Asylum-seekers and refugees are among the most vulnerable and marginalised people, many having experienced torture, trauma and other catastrophic events" Dr Jenkins

MANUS ALERT

People don't realise that there are also about 120 refugees and asylum seekers brought from Manus Island and Naura to Port Moresby for medical care. They have these horrible, horrendous issues they are in very hot and very humid conditions and suffering skin conditions, kidney stones and urinary infections from not getting enough water. Living almost five years in a canvas tent. ... depression is another major issue, compounded by the unending uncertainty about their fate. They don't get told what is happening next. The men describe it as a new form of torture.

Big moment of happiness and sadness in the prison camps.Those who received their results today were so excited that they will fly to the USA on 12 of Jan 2018 and the others in camps are so sad because their names not on the list. I hope everyone will get his freedom to safe country soon. (Abdul Aziz Adam, 10:20 PM - 14 Dec 2017)

MAN ON MESSENGER

MAN: United State says it is father of human rights and a democratic country but there is a travel ban policy for some Muslim countries.

Saudi Arabia and Iran are very religious countries but I never heard of travel ban policy in those countries. Even Saudi and Iran are very religious countries but they never said that "No Christian, No Buddhism, No white, No Asian ....,..."

JILL: Hey Man I will neaten this up and post it from me saying it came from a friend. I will post it again with your name once you are safely off Manus.

MAN: Thanks Aunty. It is came from my heart.

Man becomes clearer and more articulate by the day. It is wonderful to watch. Yes Man I also wonder how America will embrace you.

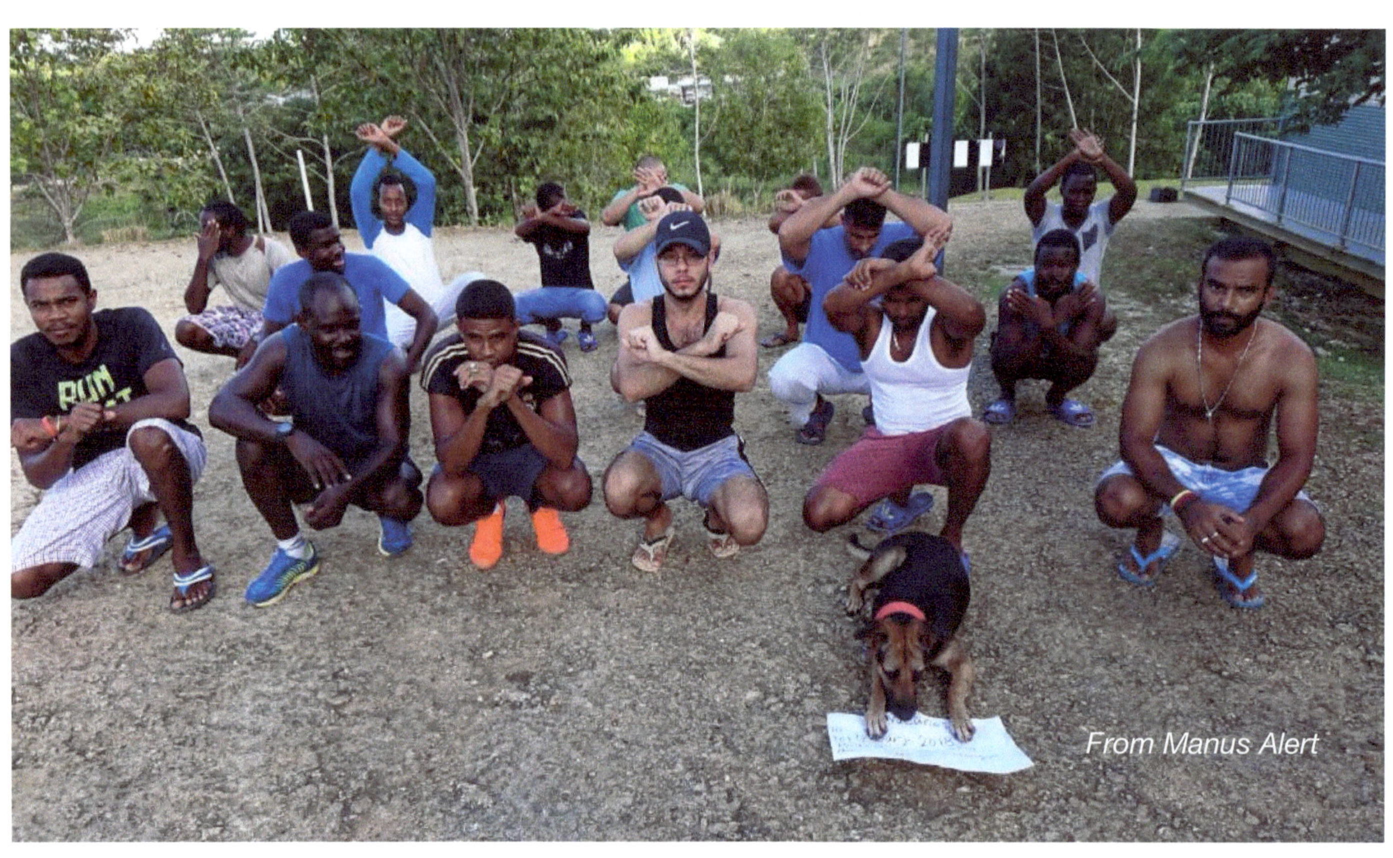
From Manus Alert

"Manus Island police use metal poles to beat refugees and asylum seekers. Papua New Guinean police have used batons to beat refugees and asylum seekers in the Manus Island detention centre, as they continue operation physically moving refugees out of the centre".
Behrouz Boochani

MANUS ALERT   MAN ON MESSENGER

Four big things from PNG Supreme Court today:
• Asylum seekers who opted out of the Slater and Gordon case are eligible for payment in PNG for the breaches of their human rights.
• In February, PNG lawyers will seek that the Australian and PNG government provide a safe, third country for the asylum seekers unlawfully sent to Manus Island.
• PNG Supreme Court on 5 February will examine human rights breaches in the siege of, and forced eviction from, the Manus detention centre at Lombrum. (Thurs 23 Oct & Black Friday attacks).
• The judge suggested that damages (compensation payment) be sought for the human rights breaches associated with the eviction from Lombrum and for the on-going breaches associated with the inadequate and inhuman conditions in Waste Haus, East & Hellside.
PNG Supreme Court rules major victory to Manus asylum seekers (Refugee Action Coalition) December 15, 2017)

MAN: 50 % is happy ,50 % is upset for myself
Not 100%
So sad for my friends.
I lived with them.
They have very good heart.
Just rumor Muslim and Middle Easter are anger, attackers and terrorists.

JILL: You will miss them of course and want them safe too.

MAN: I'm sad it's not for separated with them.
Just I'm sad for they are still in hell and hopeless especially for Middle Eastern and Muslim.

JILL: Yes it is sad. I am so sad too. I wish Manus was emptied of those in detention and that they all had freedom to start new lives.

MAN: Dear Australian friends!!! Please look after to Abu Sayed. When I leave from this country. He needs your helps . He is a sick man.
Then please try to get him out of from this hell.
Manus is very dangerous for him.. I'll concern about him at all until he already been settled in safe country .

I empathise fully with Man's concern for his friend and am so concerned for Abu but how can I or other advocates help when we do not speak Abu's language and he can't understand ours. He also does not write.

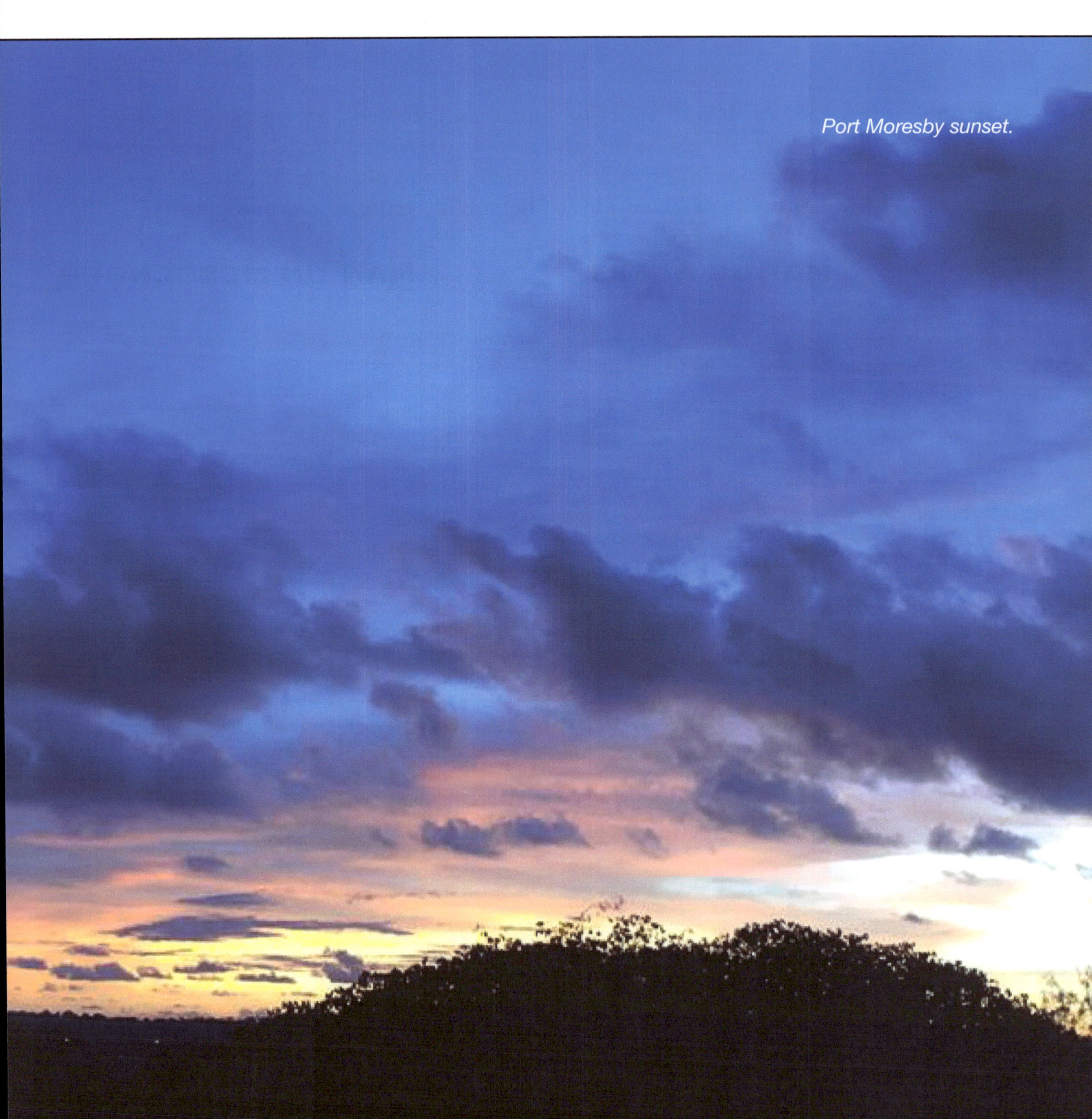
Port Moresby sunset.

"Manus Island: MSF denied access to refugees as thousands rally in Australia. The protest has caused significant traffic delays around the port. Victoria Police are at the site". The Guardian

MANUS ALERT

This morning the management began to issue mobile phones and they just issued around 70 phones. Most of the guys were extremely frustrated as they waited 2 hours but didn't get phones. We have lack facilities in west camp. We're fed up with this system Ples stop torturing us (Shamindan tweet) There are about 170 men in Waste Haus #Manus. So about 100 men did not get the phones & credit they were supposed to receive the day they moved into Waste. Waiting up to 6 weeks so far. Dutton said everything was ready for us.

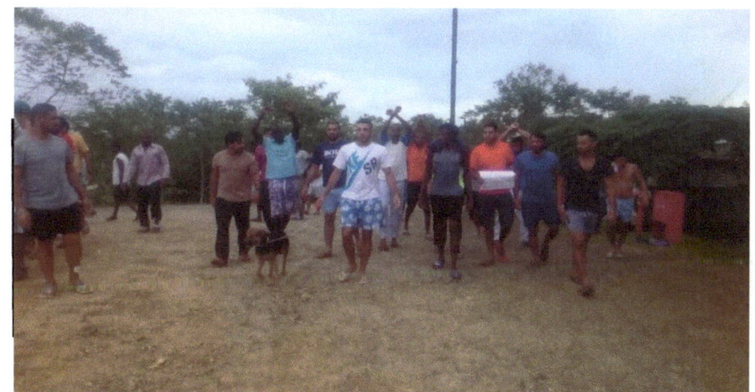

MAN ON MESSENGER

MAN: Hi my aunty. Your gift (photo book) is with me to USA .. I brought it from manus

JILL: Great. Once you send me your new address I will send you your second book there. I hope you remember the good and leave the bad behind when you go.

MAN: Aunty I met with a lot of bad things in manus, but they are useful things for my future.
I thought that four and half years is too long when I was in Manus, but now I think four and a half years is just a while.

JILL: Yes we'll take the best and use it

MAN: The life is too short.

JILL: Well now you will be free to make the best of life.

MAN: I'll aunty. Thanks for treating me so friendly and warmly.

JILL: You will always be a friend Man.

MAN: Thanks again

JILL: Thank you.

MAN: Sometime I thought that I cloud be dead if I didn't meet with you all.

I am deeply touched by Man's thanks. It is great to be recognised and immensely satisfying to know that I have made his life a little easier. He is a very easy person to care about. "Thank you Man knowing you brings me great joy".
There is change on Manus. Management of the detention centres gets more chaotic by the day, the men's physical and mental wellbeing deteriorates but their capacity to resist together grows.

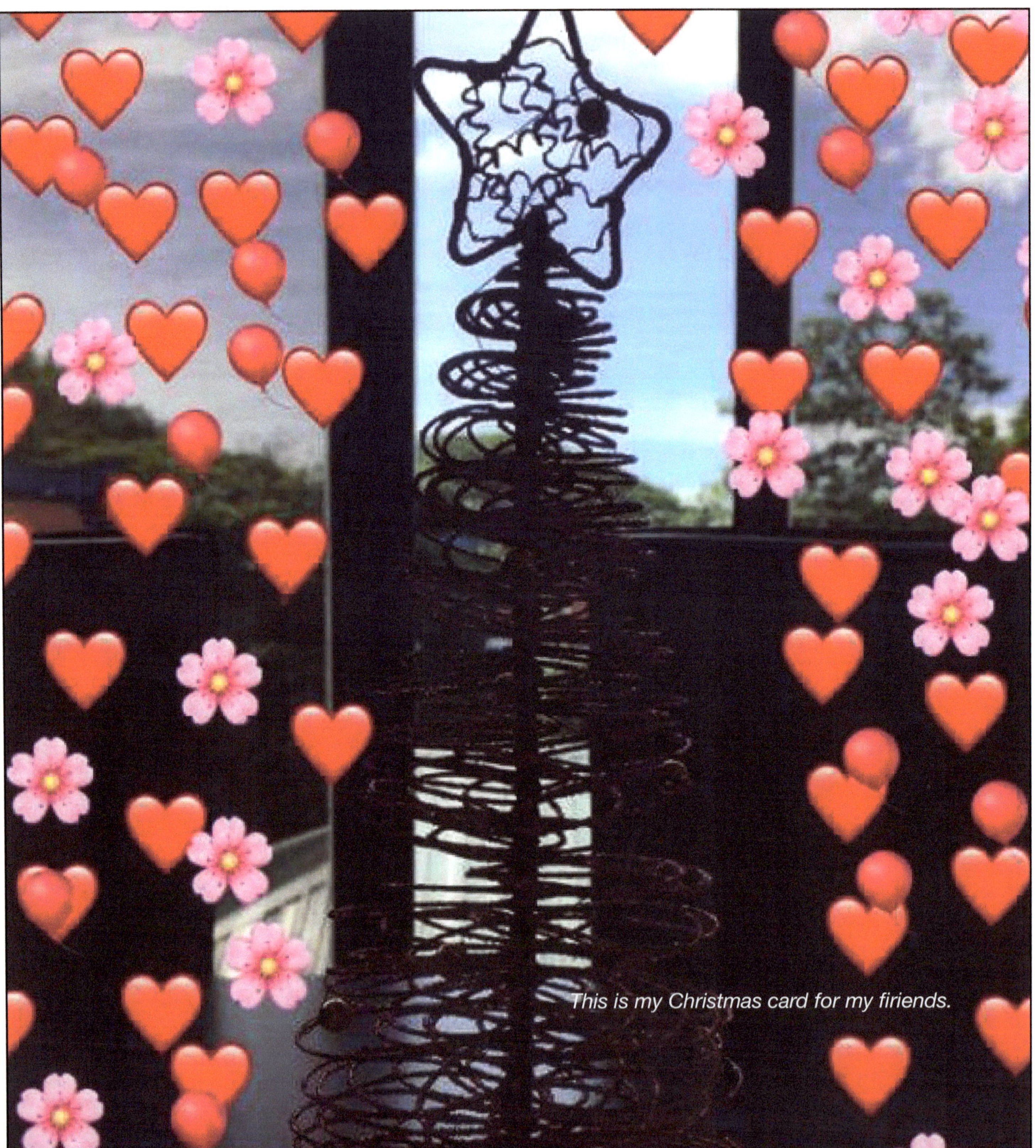
This is my Christmas card for my firiends.

"Protesters block the gates of refugee accommodation on Manus Island, stopping staff from entering, refugees leaving and supplies from reaching the centre". The Guardian

MANUS ALERT

MAN ON MESSENGER

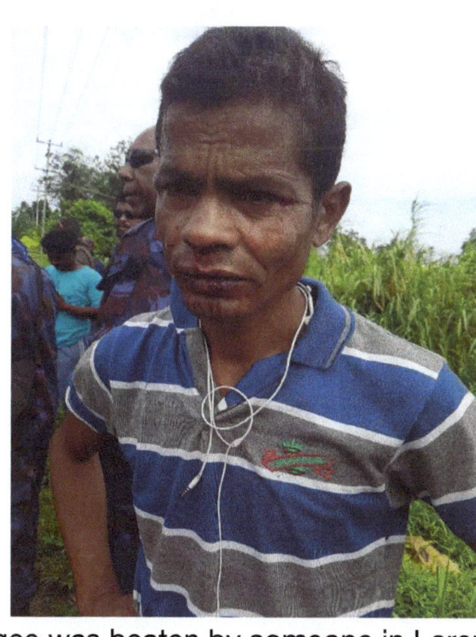

A refugee was beaten by someone in Lorengau market an hour ago. They hit his face, and as he was giving information to police his face was bleeding. Most of the refugees prefer to stay in their rooms to prevent more situations like this. #Manus (Behrouz Boochani 11:55 AM - 18 Dec 2017)

MAN: Morning Aunty
I have been asking Abu. He is very happy and thanked for your help.
Please just let me know what do you need his details?? Aunty he is a sick man . Thanks again for him.
He has heart problems.He was in Mainland detentions for one and half years.Then ABF sent back him to here .. he is unwell and his medication is also not easy to get in Manus.

JILL: Ok.

Man: He is a Rogingan (Stateless, Rogingan, Rohingan.
Thanks Aunty please ask me if you need more details.

MAN: Hi Aunty After three weeks we leave to US. Some people got result. We don't have to going back to Manus but I'll update you with more information tomorrow when I came back from my appointment.

Man's keen awareness of the plight of his fellow detainees was evidenced in previous comments on why he stayed for three weeks of hunger strikes when all detainees were told to leave the Lombrum Centre. Now as the reality of leaving PNG sinks in, Man is steeped in survivor guilt. This is contagious when he speaks about Abu. I read again about the danger for detainees in PNG, feel helpless, but try to follow through on Man's request anyway.
Dutton rushes to "clear backlogs" in visa processing to "free" Australia of "illegals" and offloads offshore detention centres onto the poor countries who host them. The billions spent by his department grow.

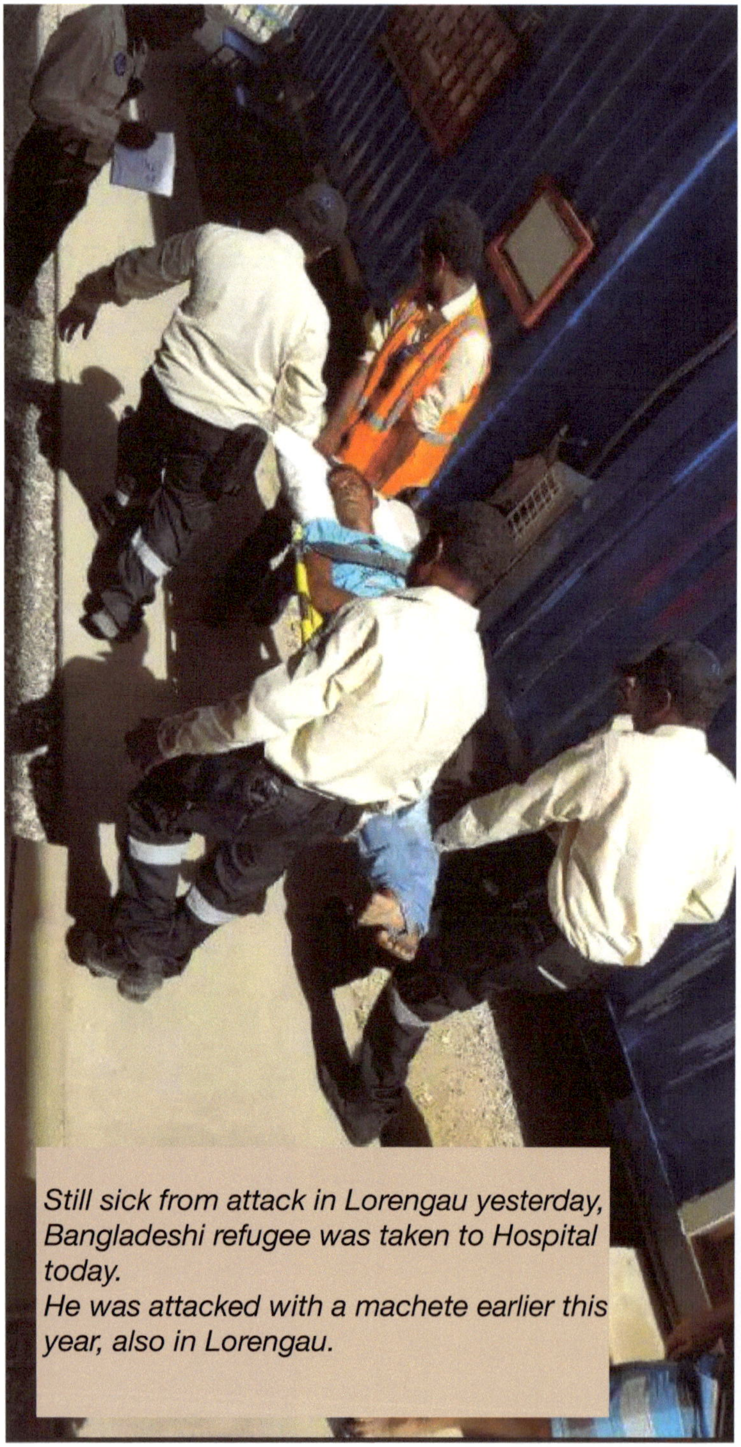

Still sick from attack in Lorengau yesterday, Bangladeshi refugee was taken to Hospital today.
He was attacked with a machete earlier this year, also in Lorengau.

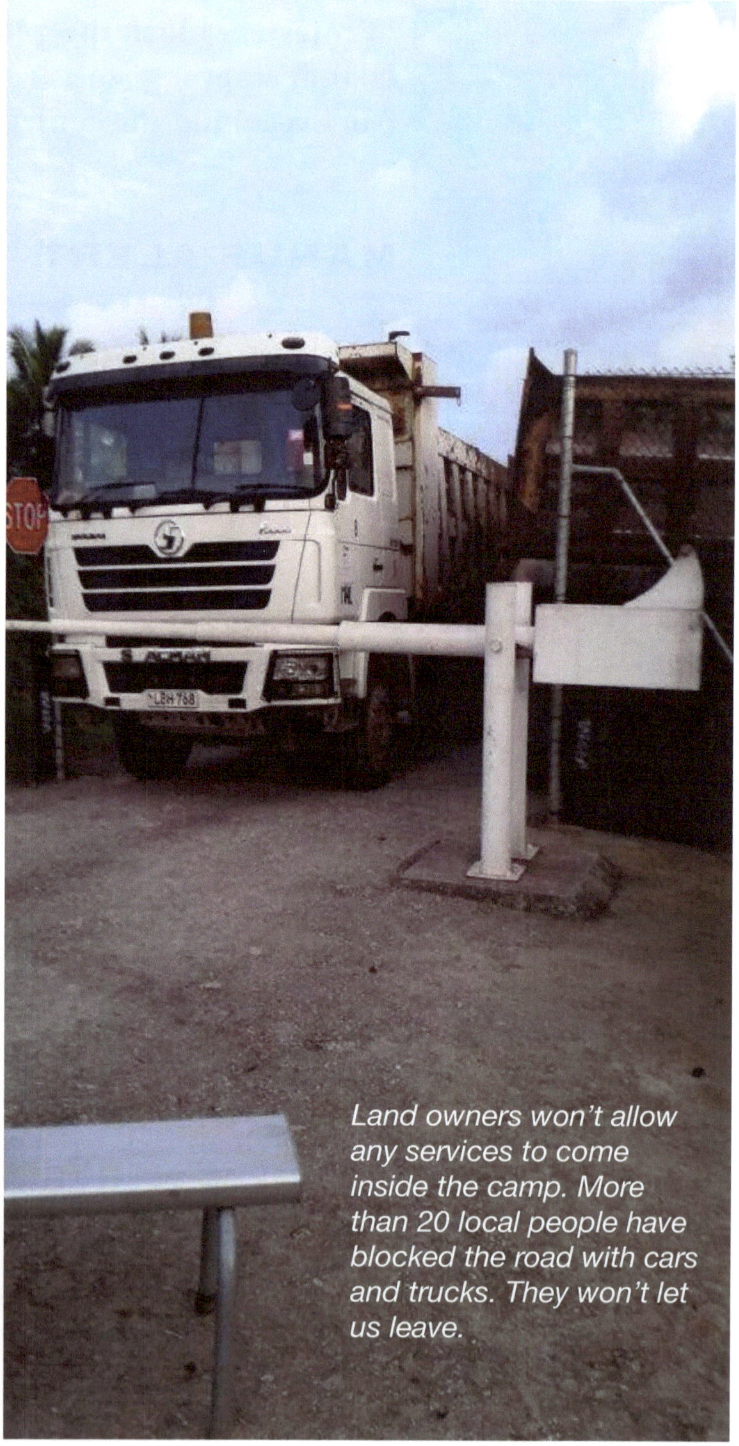

Land owners won't allow any services to come inside the camp. More than 20 local people have blocked the road with cars and trucks. They won't let us leave.

<table>
<tr><td>

19 DEC 2017

</td><td>

"Refugees on Manus Island say they are running out of food because local landowners are blockading their accommodation. ... landowners have been stopping staff, medicine and food deliveries from going in to the East Lorengau Transit Centre, where more than 300 men are kept". ABC News

</td></tr>
</table>

MANUS ALERT   MAN ON MESSENGER

Last night a local leader said, 'please tell all ELRTC refugees don't came outside. It's not safe for all refugees.

Today The land owners are protesting against IHMS, ABF, ICSA and JDA caseworkers. More than 20 local people have blocked the road with cars and trucks. They won't allow any services to come inside the camp.

If those services stop then how will we survive?

We can't go outside and if we try they will beat us. Nobody is allowed in or out. One refugee was going out and they stopped him by pulling a knife.

The local people blocking the road to East Lorengau Transit are shouting and threatening refugees who try to go out for hospital appointments or to buy for their needs.

We are really scared. Please help us and pray for us.

ELRTC = East Lorengau Refugee Transit Centre
IHMS = International Health and Medical Services
ABF   = Australian Border Force
ICSA   = PNG's Immigration and Citizenship Advisory Service
JDA   = workforce of JDA an Australian organisation.

MAN: You may think that I'm a very isolationist but you won't be know about single's feeling and life.
No worries
No attachment
No responsibility
No review and unaccountable No are just available for only single life.
What I want I could
What I don't want I don't need
Just I Want to live as single life for the whole my life.
Love ?? Just I need part timers love
Entertainment? Just for movement
Caring ? Just for awhile
Visiting? Just for a few days
Responsibility? Not more than a few hours
Everything is just for part time
If I want I'll
If I can't I won't be.

No wonder Man believes in keeping himself independent and free of attachment. It is exhausting to care. I wonder if he will change when he truly feels free and safe. Will he ever risk attachment? As the physical and mental wellbeing of men still on Manus deteriorates, advocates focus more on individuals. Back in Australia there are still marches, rallies and sit-ins, and civil disobedience has grown. Many comment on the government's move towards totalitarianism, but a sense of hopelessness blankets activity. I see in myself and in other advocates the toll of caring. We are becoming ragged after years of fighting.

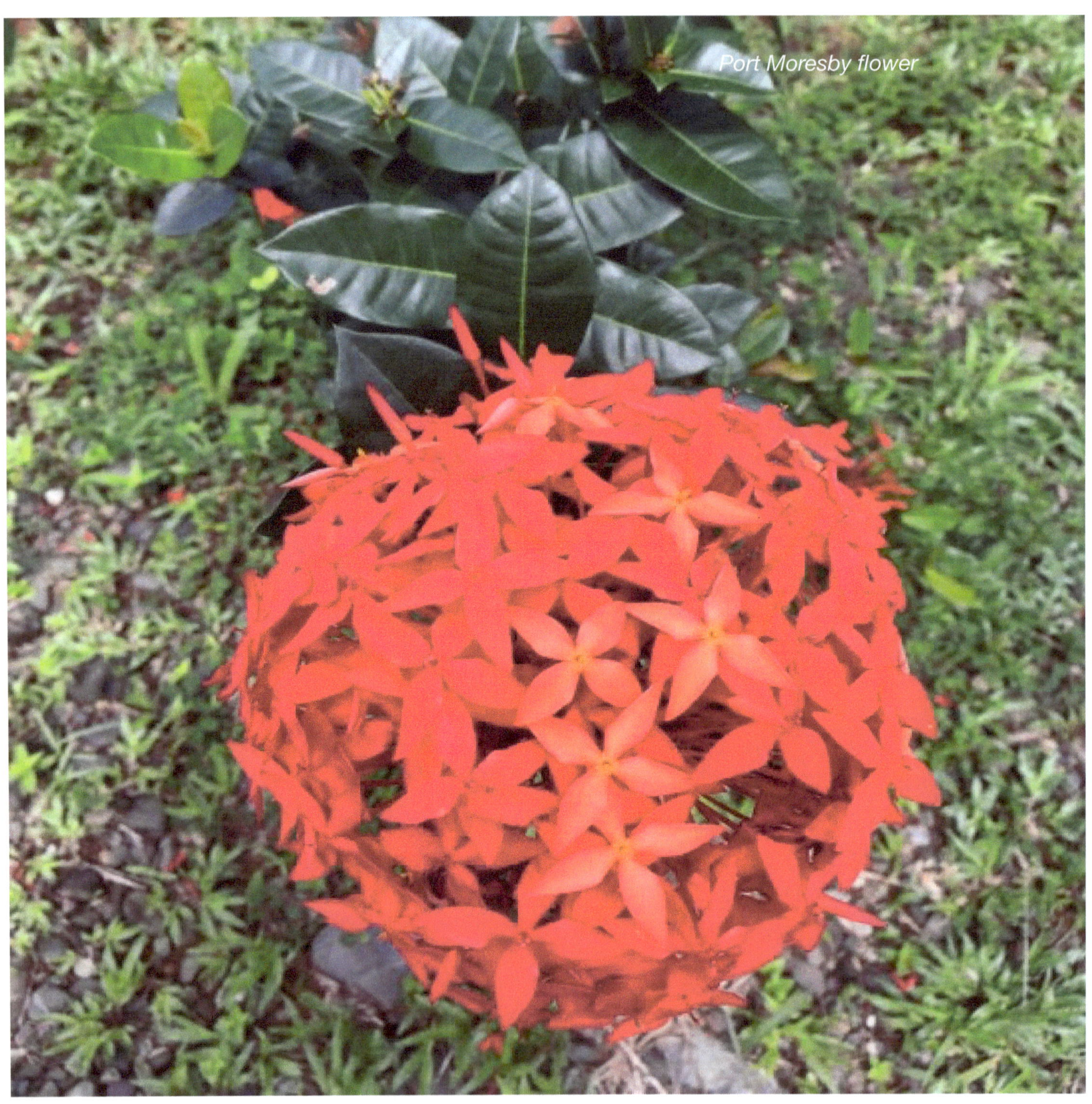
Port Moresby flower

"The federal government refused a senate request to release documents regarding the construction of the new Australian-built asylum seeker facilities on Manus Island. The request seeks detail about the health, construction and security provisions". The Guardian

MANUS ALERT

MAN ON MESSENGER

General Notice

Date: 18-12-2017

This is to notify all residents living at West Hill Compounds, there won't be any appointments for today at IHMS due to the events occurring at ELRTC.

Until the matter is resolved should you then be advice to keep safe until further notice.

We will keep you informed and updated if situation is back and operating normally

By Management

No IHMS today. Cancelled. Land owners won't allow any services to come inside the camps. Local landowners have blocked ELRTC road & won't allow IHMS inside. IHMS works in ELRTC.

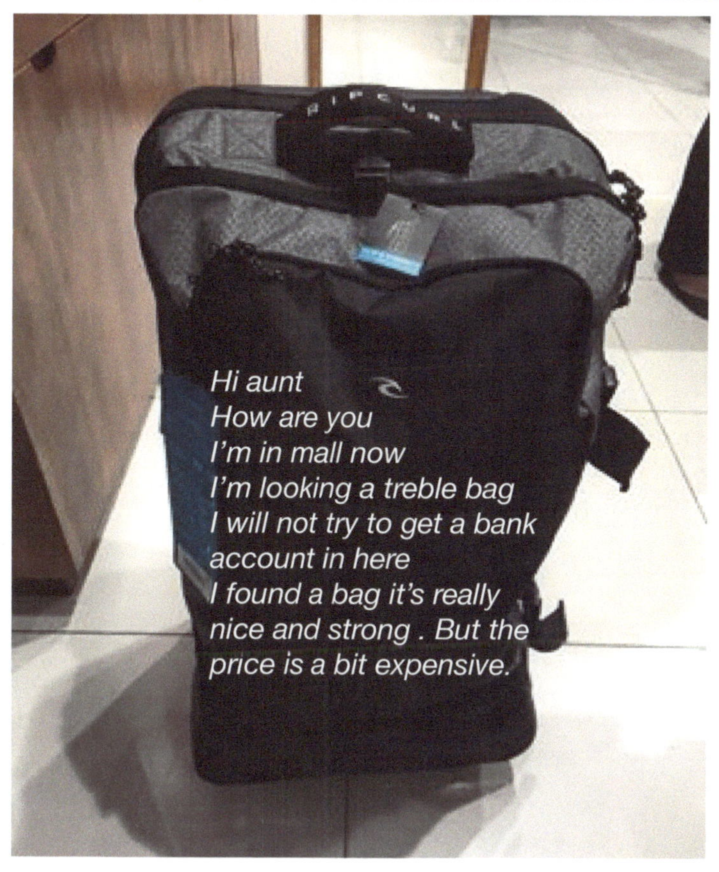

Man seems to be moving to a different place. His excitement is palpable as he shares his search for a suitable bag to carry his small reminders of the horror on Manus. "I will always remember my good friends".
On Manus dysfunction builds daily but the resolve of detainees grows as they share each duty of care breach with the world.

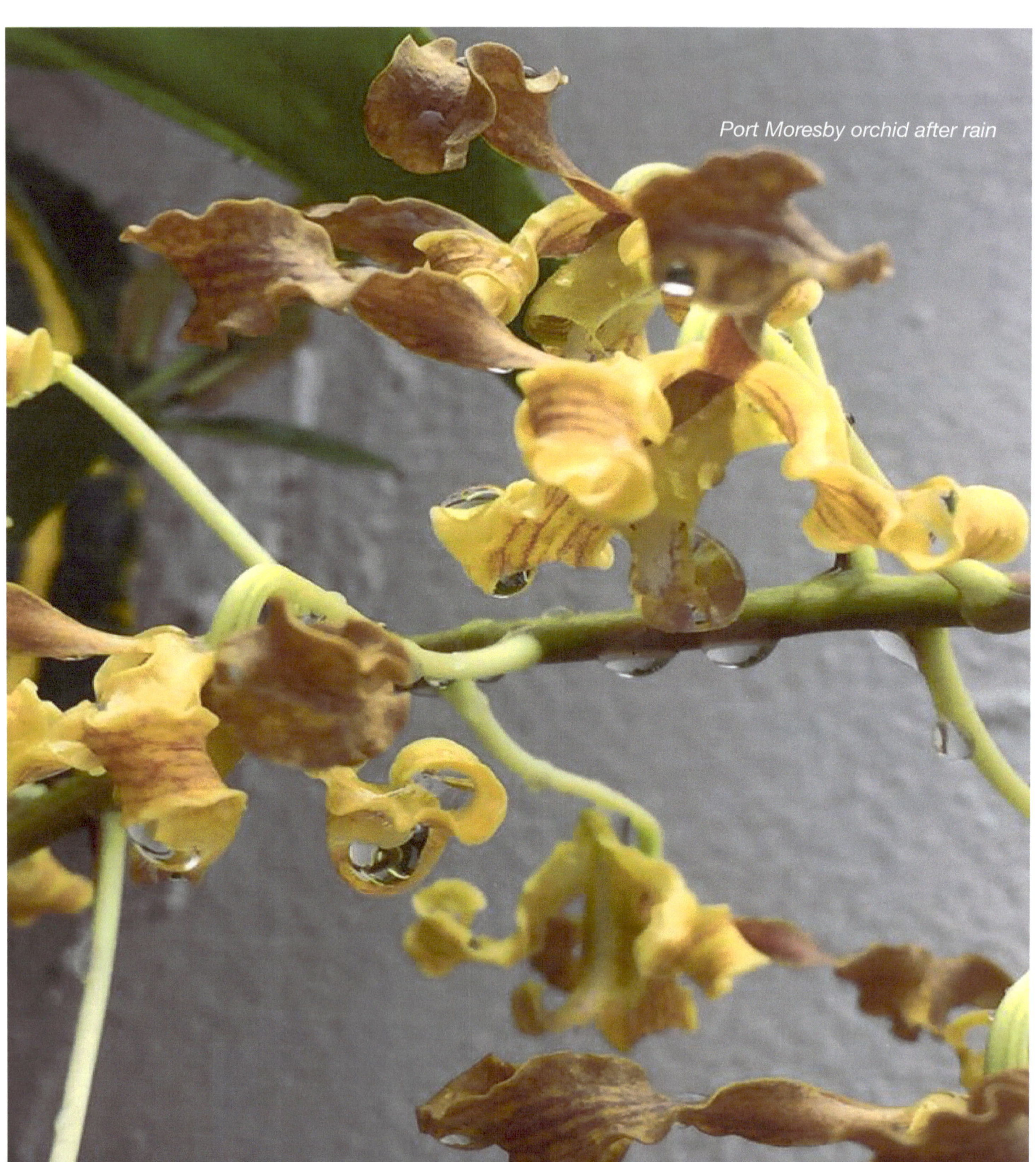
Port Moresby orchid after rain

"Australian Christian Churches call for compassion for refugees. Our political "leaders" pose as Christians, but look at their intentional cruelty to refugees. At Christmas time, too". Julian Burnside

MANUS ALERT   MAN ON MESSENGER

REQUEST:
We Hillside House asylum seekers have not received any services for four weeks.
According to the information you provided to us at the previous camp, we should have canteen and phone services here.
West and East Lorengau camps have received all those services together but nobody is accountable for our problems.
Please consider our problems.
Attached: 35 signatures of Hillside Haus asylum seekers.

MAN: Aunty
I allocated to my crocheted stuffs for my favorite person. if someone Australian is coming to Manus please let me know. I would like give it for you. It may my last gift because I don't know yet what will happen in US. I may have time to crochet or not that's why I would like give my crafts to my favorite friends.

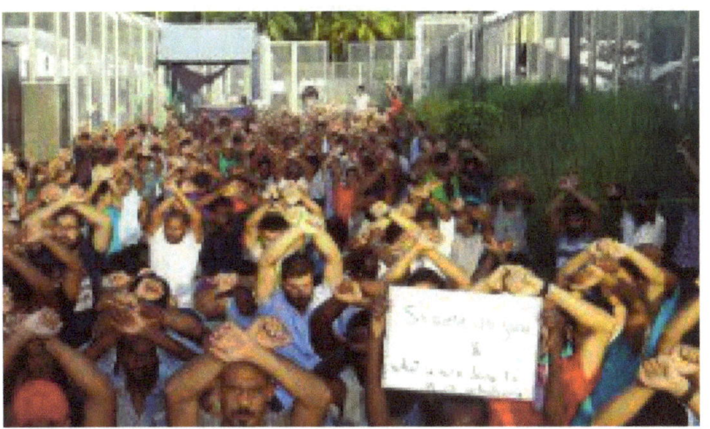

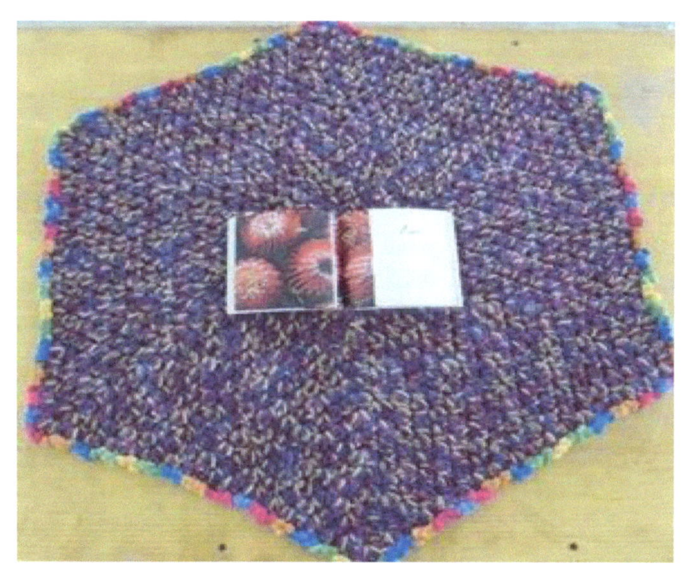

As Man gets closer to leaving he is divesting himself of connections to Manus. He is also looking forward and beginning to think about what his future might hold. I treasure that I am one of the people he wishes to entrust with the product of his creativity. For me this is a token of thanks for sharing his journey.

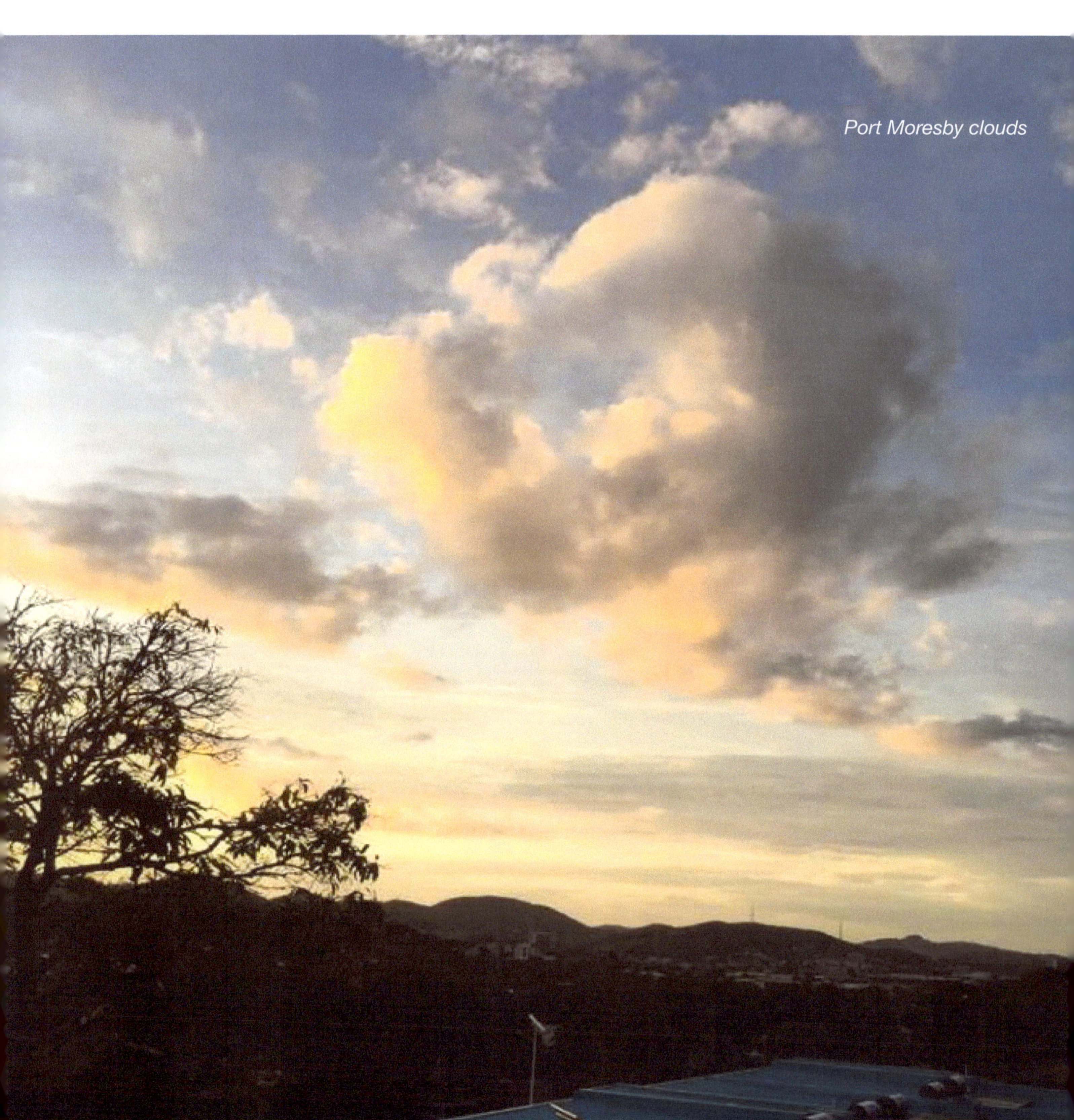
Port Moresby clouds

MANUS ALERT   MAN ON MESSENGER

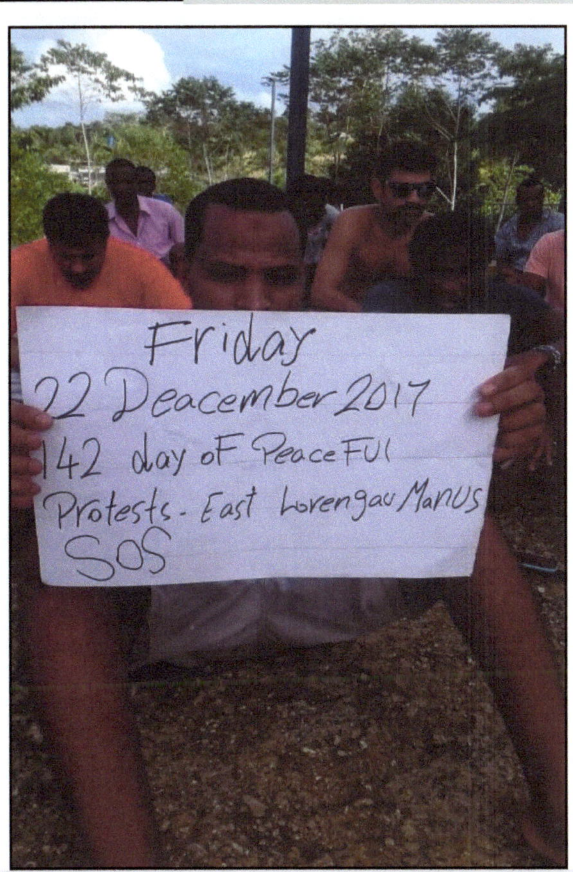

MAN: Hi Aunty. My friends they said that Now Transit Center is just same as Lomburm. No one can go out.

JILL: So pleased you aren't there.

MAN: Thanks again. But I'm a bit sad for them. I hope so that they are OK Aaunty. Tonight only I'll ring to Abu but there's an uncertain place Could be happen at anytime.

JILL: Yes it is an unhappy dangerous place.

MAN: Aunt I dreamt about my parents.

JILL: Oh is that the first time Man. Were they safe in your dream?

MAN: It's not the first time but very seldom dream about them. Yes they're ok in my dream.
....(long silence)

JILL: Good I hope your dreams bring peace.

MAN: Thank you Aunty.

So Eaten Fish is free thank God and Man is beginning to allow himself to process things from long ago. I know that Man will prosper.
I wonder how long it will take for him to separate from the hell where he was for all those years. It is excruciating to tell him that I as advocate can do nothing further for Abu.
There are times that I dream of simply turning my back on this horrendous mess.

'Eaten Fish' (who was detained on Manus) is the name Ali Durrani called himself in his work as a cartoonist.

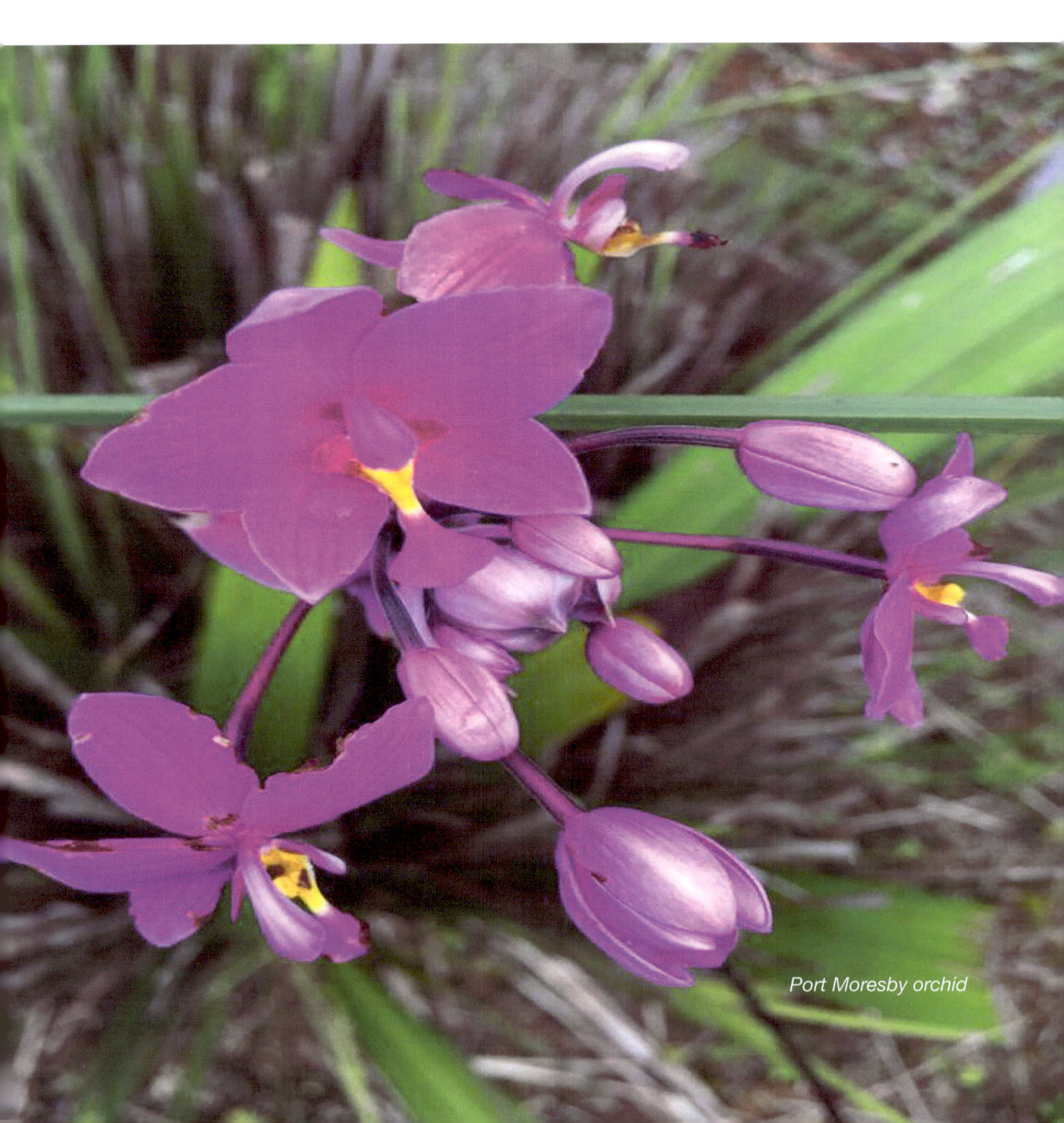

Port Moresby orchid

<table>
<tr><td>

23 DEC 2017

</td><td>

"Australia to fix Manus Island refugee 'mess' as hundreds toil in unsafe camps. PRESSURE has been placed on the government to solve the refugee crisis on Manus Island as the UN calls for Australia to take responsibility for the 'mess'." Reuters

</td></tr>
</table>

MANUS ALERT

Yesterday, asylum seekers & refugees who are sick & waiting for treatment in Port Moresby gathered in front of Wilson Security office to demand their rights including a weekly allowance & other necessities. Then the Australian Wilson Security guards left the office. They have not returned today. They left because they had no answers to our questions. Because Wilson Security have gone, some sick people missed their medical appointments. Some are feeling terrible because of this.

The situation is desperate for us. Most of us sell our food, juice & milk because we need money to buy necessities.

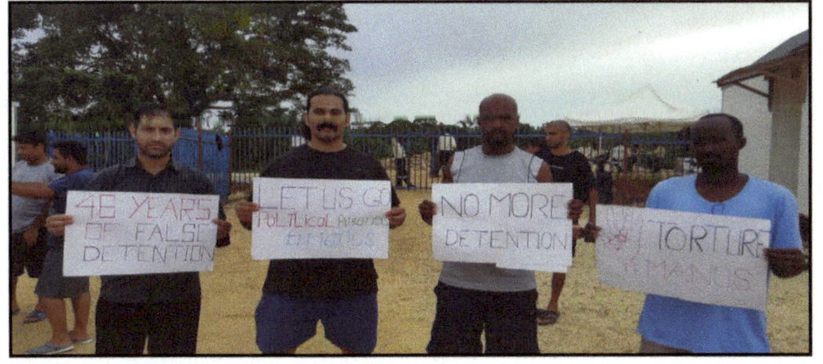

MAN ON MESSENGER

MAN: Thanks a lot for helping us.

JILL: My pleasure.

I received my lovely gift today – think you Lim you are too kind. The top is just lovely and I think I will wear it tomorrow. Looking forward to reading the book Much love and many thanks xx

This is a thank you note from Man's Caseworker.

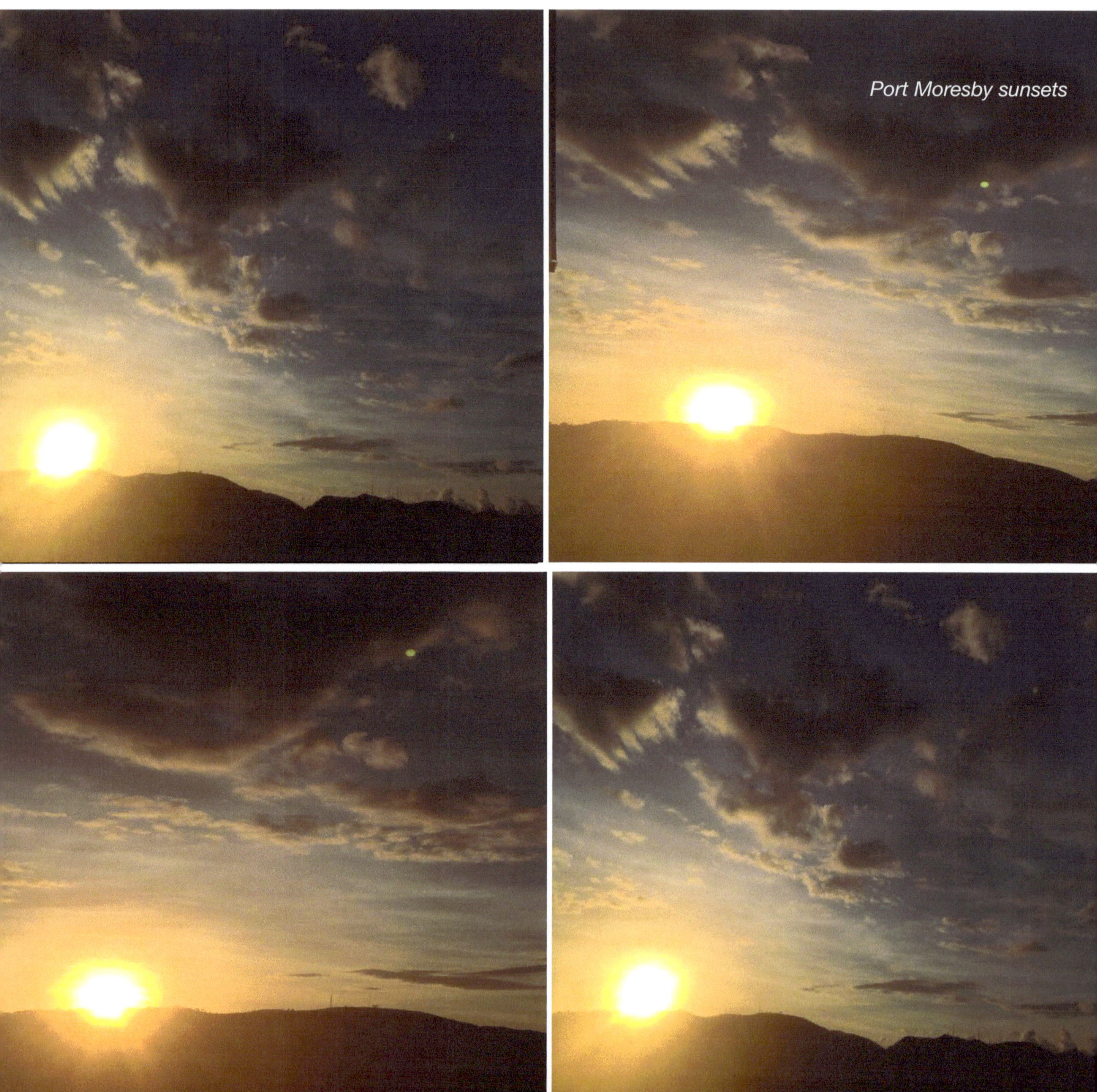
Port Moresby sunsets

"Another problem at West Haus & Hillside today. Since early morning Manus company 'Kingfisher Security' preventing Paladin security guards from going in & has control of camps. ..." Behrouz Boochani

MANUS ALERT   MAN ON MESSENGER

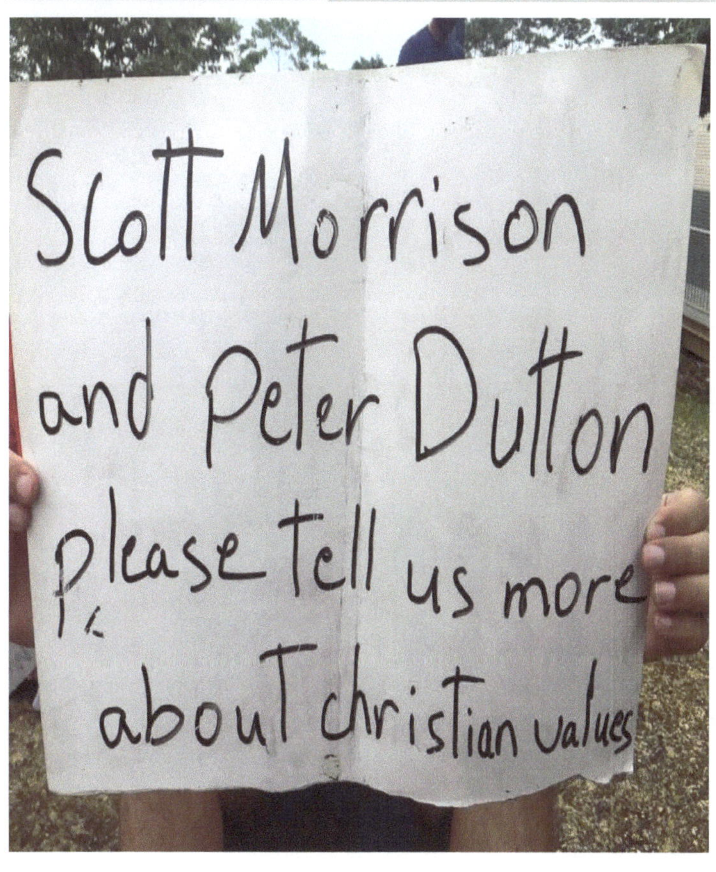

It's my present for your grandchildren Aunty.

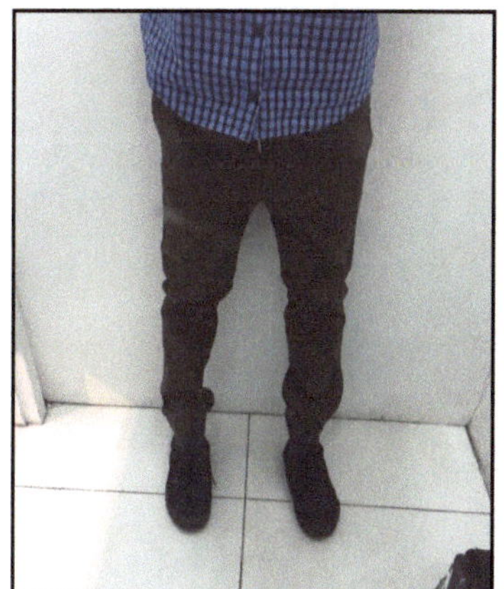

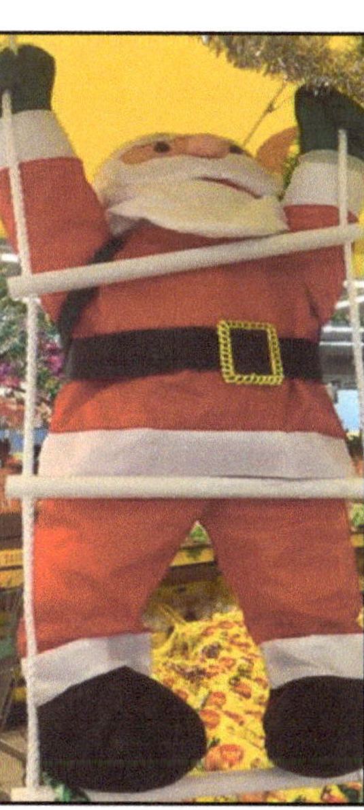

MAN: Just tired window shopping. I was feeling a bit taller than normal when I was try it. But PNG is very expensive that's why I didn't buy anything.

That pants is 147 Kinars after off but DG brand.
Yes I don't want to buy anything in here.
How are you and your grandchildren aunty ??

JILL: I am very well.

I love watching Man enjoying experiences we, who live as free citizens in a prosperous society, take for granted. I smile as I imagine him trying on his first pair of stylish jeans. It is wonderful to read his joke about "Armani outfits" at Dutton's expense. I love his Christmas present. I hate that Australia has forgotten "it's Christian values".

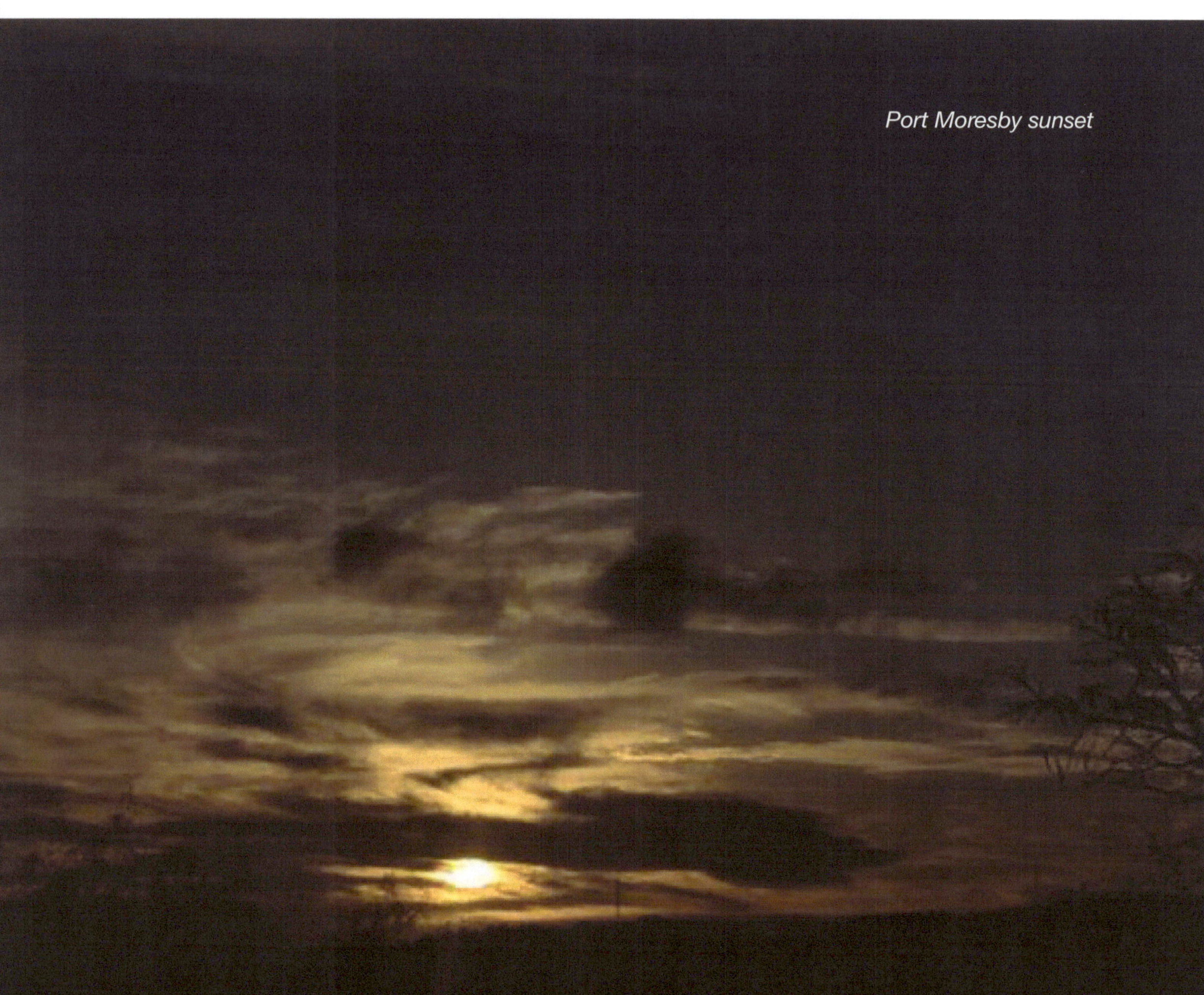
Port Moresby sunset

"On Manus Island, "refugees show greater humanity than Australia" The 24-day protest by refugees on Manus Island symbolises solidarity against oppression as they demand the freedom that Australia continues to deny". The Guardian

MANUS ALERT   MAN ON MESSENGER

I wish you and your families all a Merry Christmas Malcolm Turnbull, Petter Dutton and Bill Shorten. But don't forget while you are having a wonderful time with your family, hundreds of innocent vulnerable children, young men and women and familes are suffering for the last five years. The privilege is yours.

We have been detained for the last five years. with no crime but to serve your political career. We have sacrificed to 'protect' your borders and your inhumane policies. I remind you the the son of God Jesus was a refugee.

Six innocent men lost their lives because of your inhumane policy of border protection. We just sought your help to protect ourselves from danger but you ignored us and neglected the vulnerable innocent people.

Ask yourself, is this what you should do?

At least, please think about us in this Christmas. I pray for you and your political team to get forgiveness from your sins. Merry Christmas to you and your family. May God bless you.

Manus Prisoner

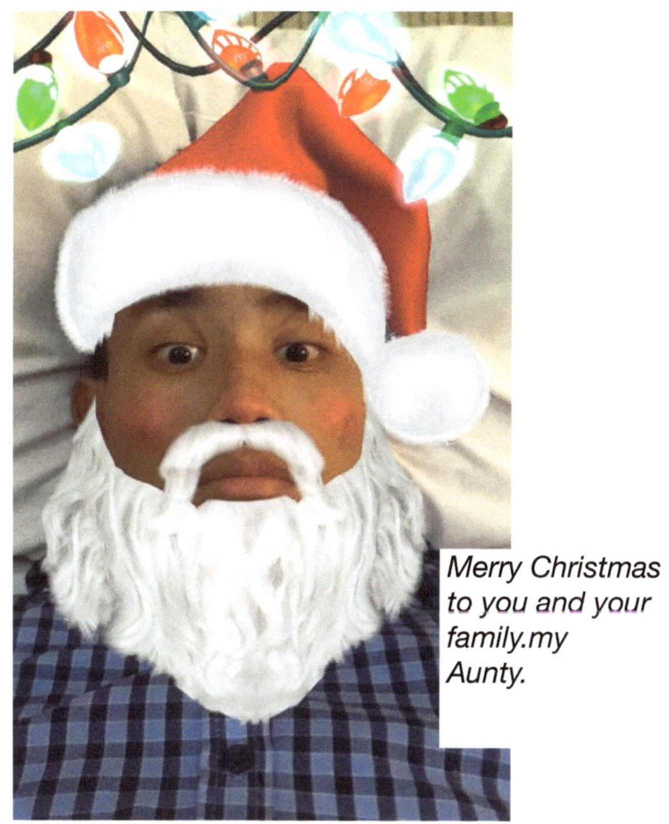

Merry Christmas to you and your family.my Aunty.

If only our government could learn from the humanity of those they incarcerate. These brave men

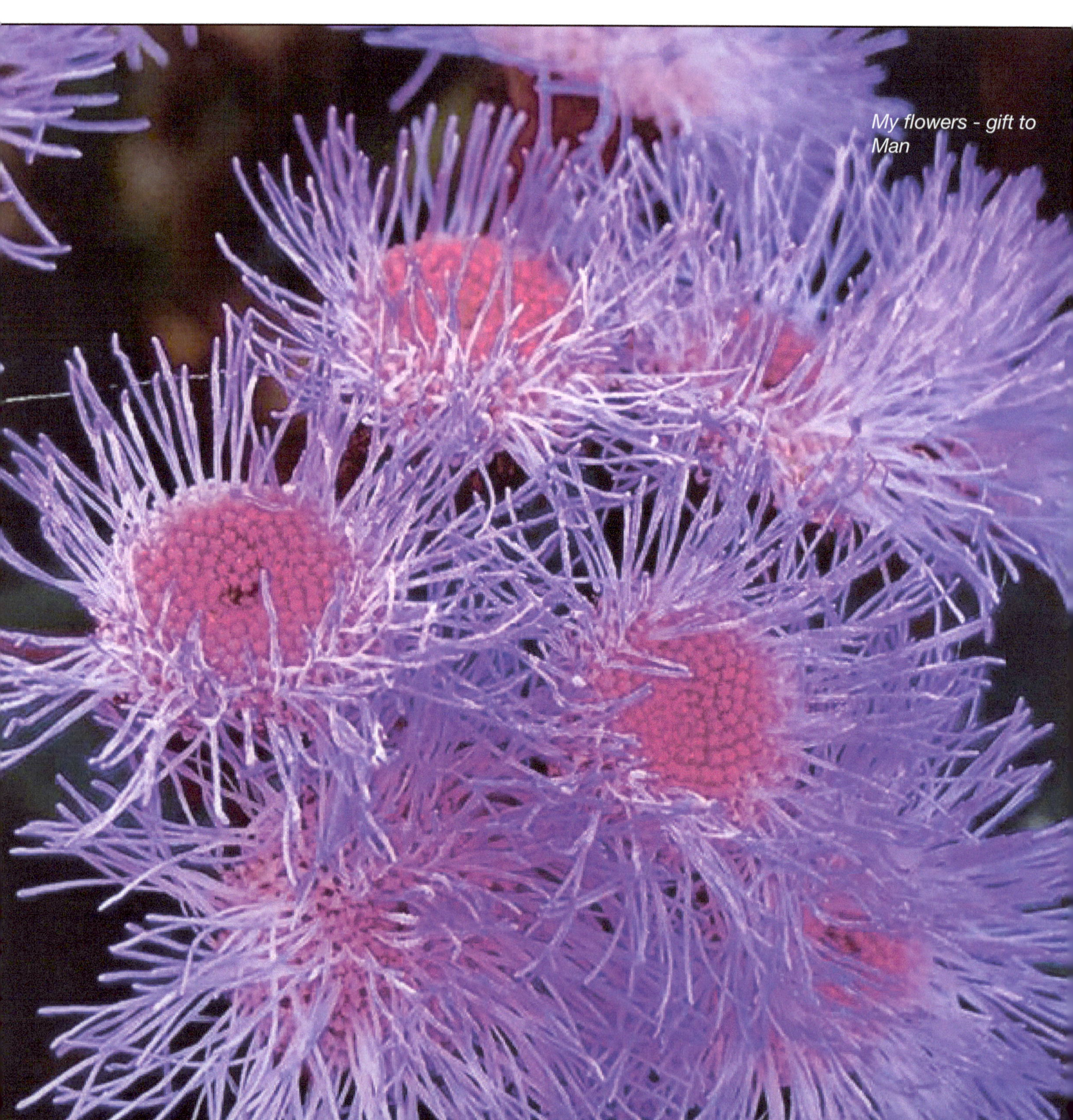
My flowers - gift to
Man

"Terrible few days. PNG immigration and police used violence to forcefully move the men onto buses and into town. Many men have been injured in the process, and there are still men without a bed in town who are sleeping on the floor in classrooms and prayer rooms".
Gifts for Manus and Nauru

MANUS ALERT

Refugee medical emergency at Lodge 10, Boroko, Port Moresby. He needs to go to hospital NOW.

Paladin, ABF & hotel manager refuse to help. Paladin security say can't help without boss permission but won't ask. ABF say they are on holiday & will take to hospital tomorrow. Hotel manager refuses to give police phone number. Refugee has been sick for days and they refused to help him. He now has extreme vomiting & diarrhoea. We have no medicine. WE NEED HELP NOW.

We are the #Manus refugees waiting to go to the USA.

26 December 2017
146th day of peaceful protests
East Lorengau Manus
SOS

MAN ON MESSENGER

MAN: Good morning aunty
Happy Boxing Day

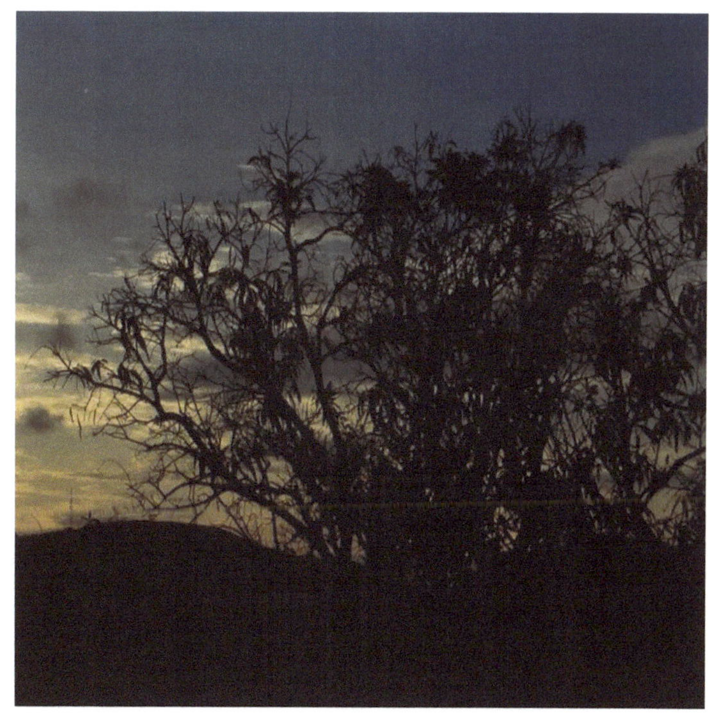

An emergency and no one responds. Even in Port Moresby. Is this mismanagement or planned dysfunction?

Gifts for Manus and Nauru supports our asylum seeker and refugee friends at Manus and Nauru.

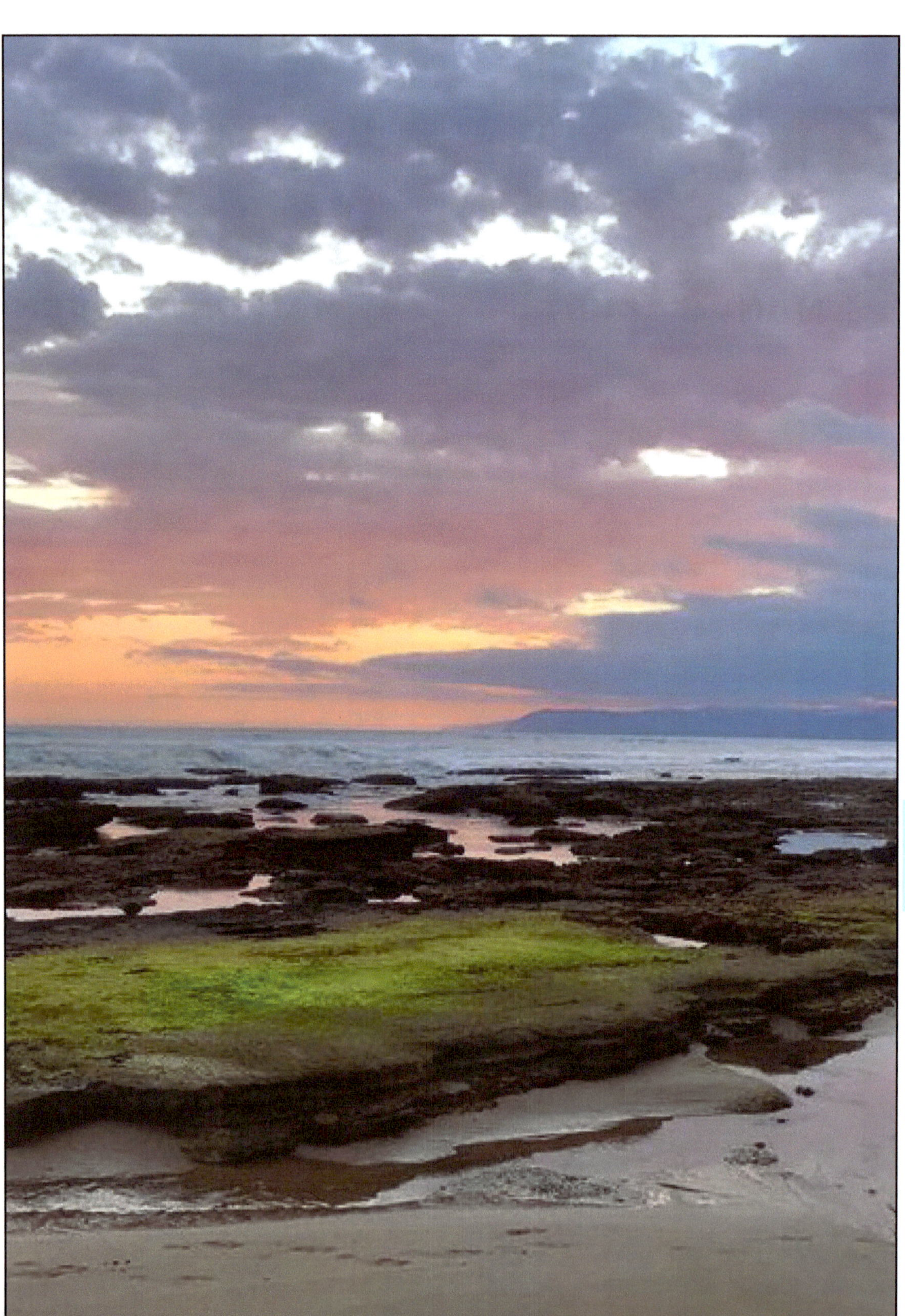

MAN: Today sunset's is not really beautiful that's why I did not take.

JILL: Mine on Fairhaven beach.

"After four years of detention on Manus Island, the author writes a poet's manifesto for the refugee resistance in which he has found himself to be a central figure 'A letter from Manus Island' from Behrouz Boochani". Refugee Action Coalition

MANUS ALERT

UN report shows health concern for Manus refugees
- Post Courier

The mission focused on the conditions and circumstances of persons of concern to UNHCR1 on Manus Island and in Port Moresby.

The delegation visited the East Lorengau Refugee Transit Centre, West Lorengau Haus and Hillside Haus accommodation sites and Lorengau General Hospital on Manus Island as well as the Granville Motel in Port Moresby.

IHMS is unable to fulfil their duty of care. They have no X-ray & no medications - only offices full of staffs. At the hospital medications are expired. Lorengau City Pharmacy don't have all our medications. There is no coordination btween IHMS & Lorengau Hospital.

MAN ON MESSENGER

JILL: Hi Man how was your day

MAN: Hi Aunty

JILL: I heard a guy in your hotel is sick. Is he OK now.

MAN: He is OK now aunty

JILL: Good I was worried for him.

MAN:: He can't says anything in here aunty because here is much different with Lomburm.
We don't have to communicate with him.

JILL: OK.

MAN: Today sunset's is not really beautiful that's why I did not take.

Another external report (UNHCR) another indictment. The Australian government appears to ignore reports wherever they come from.
Turnbull turns his attention to vilifying the Victorian premier while Dutton claims that "Sudanese gangs" are terrifying the Melbourne population who now refuse to venture into the city at night. Racism is rampant.

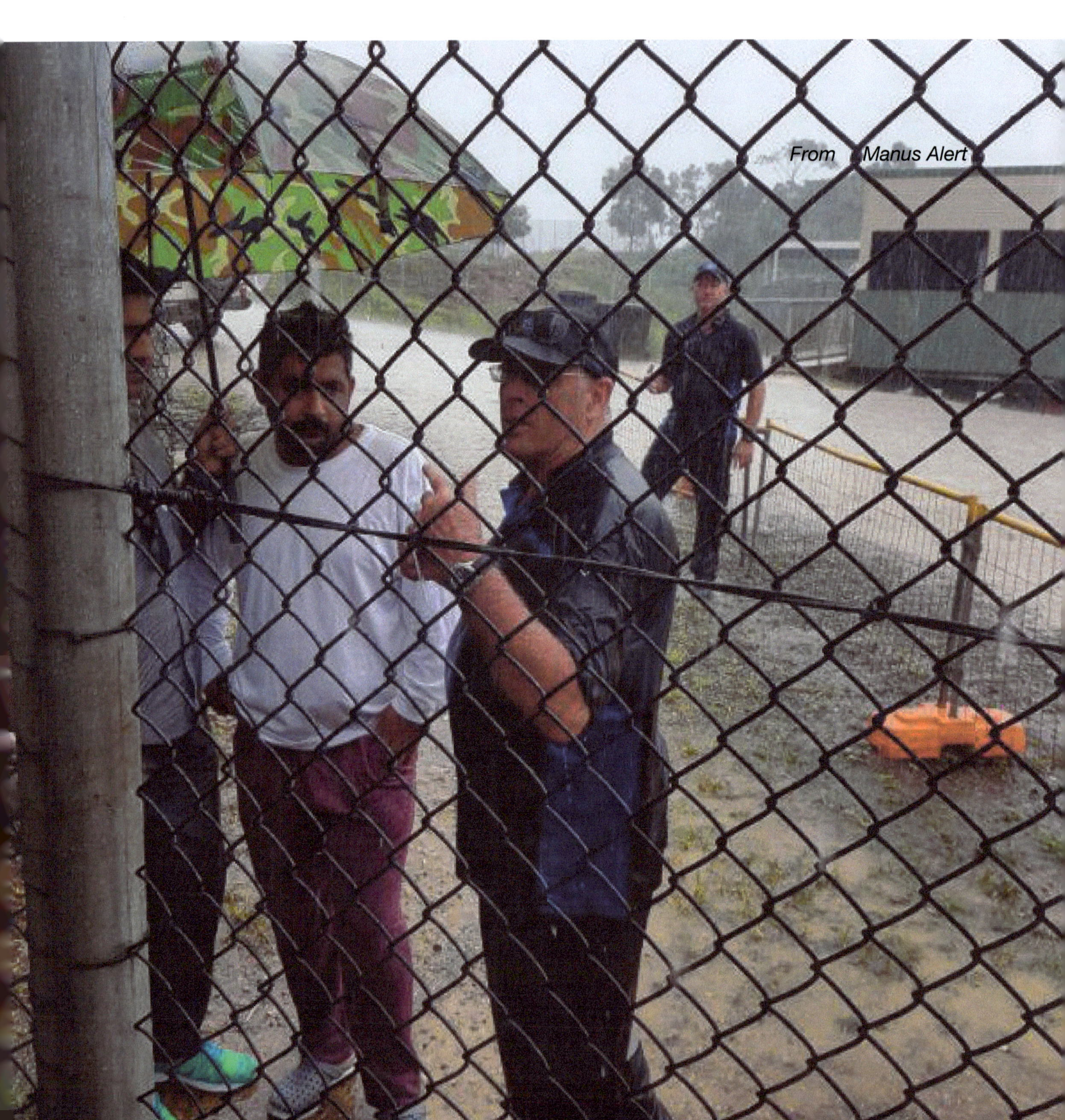
From   Manus Alert

28 DEC 2017

"A refugee advocate says asylum seekers at the Hillside Camp on Papua New Guinea's Manus Island have expelled all Australian security guards formerly employed by Wilson Security".
Radio New Zealand (RNZ)

MANUS ALERT   MAN ON MESSENGER

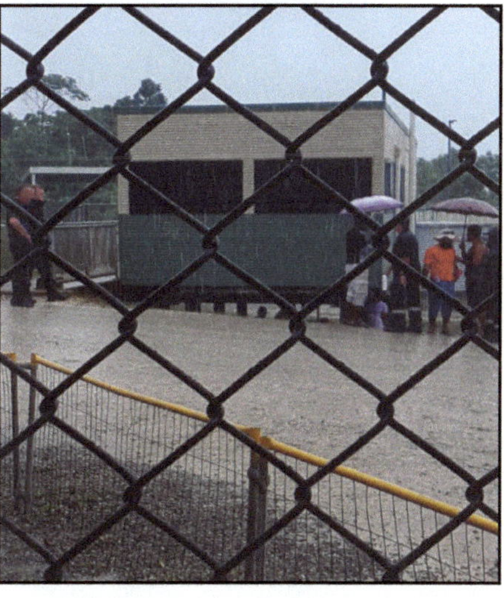

All containers leak rain water through walls & yellow bathroom water to rooms below from plumbing. Screw holes not sealed Dangerous: electrical fittings always wet.

MAN: Hi my aunty
Hope that you are well
Tonight I will go to bed an early because I have a headache.
Today I went outside for my SIM card registration.
Too hot in Pom as well
Good nigh and sweet dream.

Friday is a very important day for Muslims. We gather together to pray in congregation same as Christians congregate on a Sunday.

Paladin security today won't allow any refugees from West compound to enter the East compound to attend Friday prayers. Muslim refugees begged to go to prayer room for one hour.

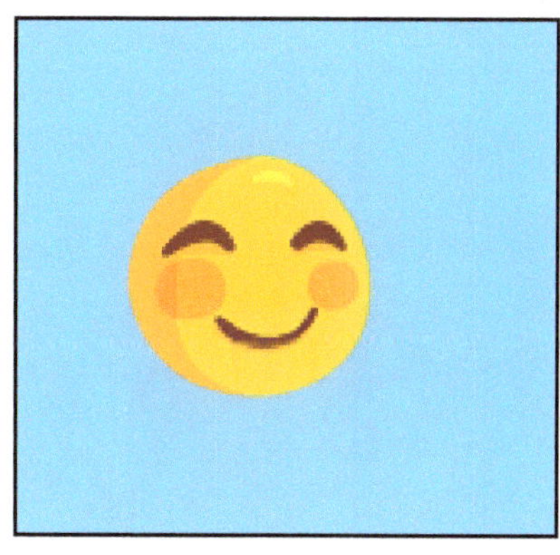

The Australian Governments move toward the creation of a homeland security department, which will incorporate immigration and border security and the Australian Federal Police. Dutton often links terrorism specifically with the Muslim religion and the LNP's Greg Hunt cites African gang crime as "out of control" in parts of Victoria and claims tougher sentencing laws are needed. On Manus detainees in West Hous are denied access to the East compound for Friday prayers. Is this a coincidence?

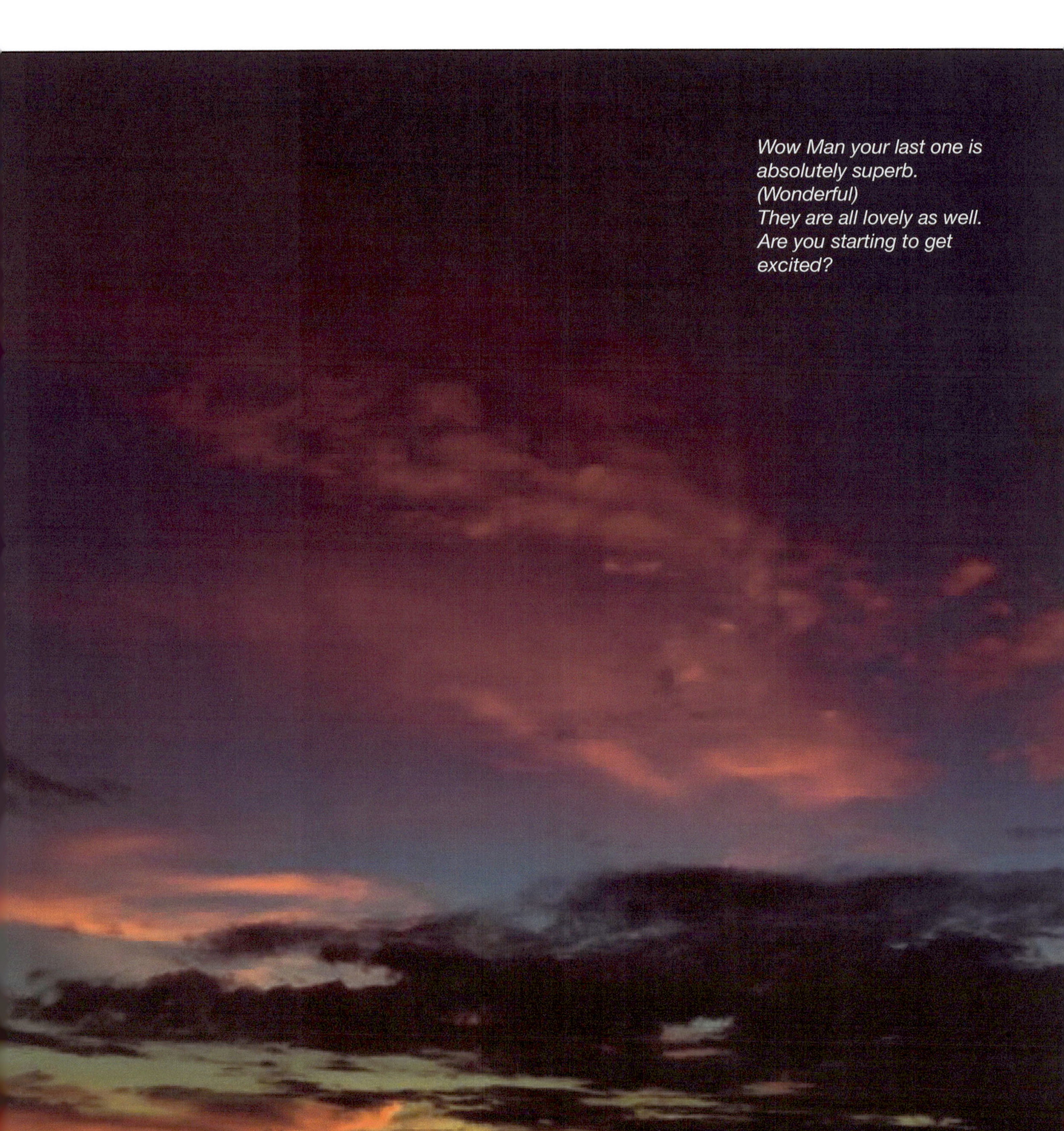
Wow Man your last one is
absolutely superb.
(Wonderful)
They are all lovely as well.
Are you starting to get
excited?

"I write from Manus Island as a duty to history. The treatment of refugees on Manus Island is part of a recurring theme of modern Australia: the annihilation and incarceration of human beings".
Behrouz Boochani

MANUS ALERT   MAN ON MESSENGER

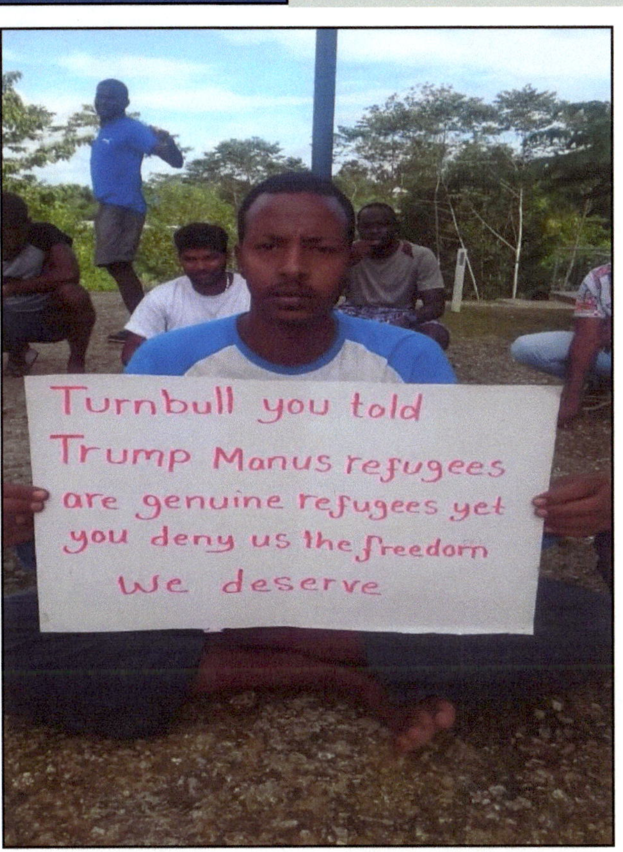

JILL: Are you starting to get excited

MAN: Excited for ??
Leaving soon
Yes but not much

JILL: Oh. I am excited for you to be out of there

MAN: Thanks aunt
We will be very far when I leave from here
USA ann Australian is too far but I'll be always contact you.

JILL: Not if you look at the world from east to west. It's not too far across the pacific and I am allowed to travel there because of good health system. Also facebook is everywhere.

MAN: Yes aunty
I want to meet you in Japan during the cherry blossom season.

JILL: Me too sounds great.

Man is now allowing himself to see some of the positives that have come out of his four and a half years in hell and begin processing his grief. I still remember my mixed feelings of relief and sorrow at leaving South Africa but it feels strange to hear some parallels between my past and Man's present.

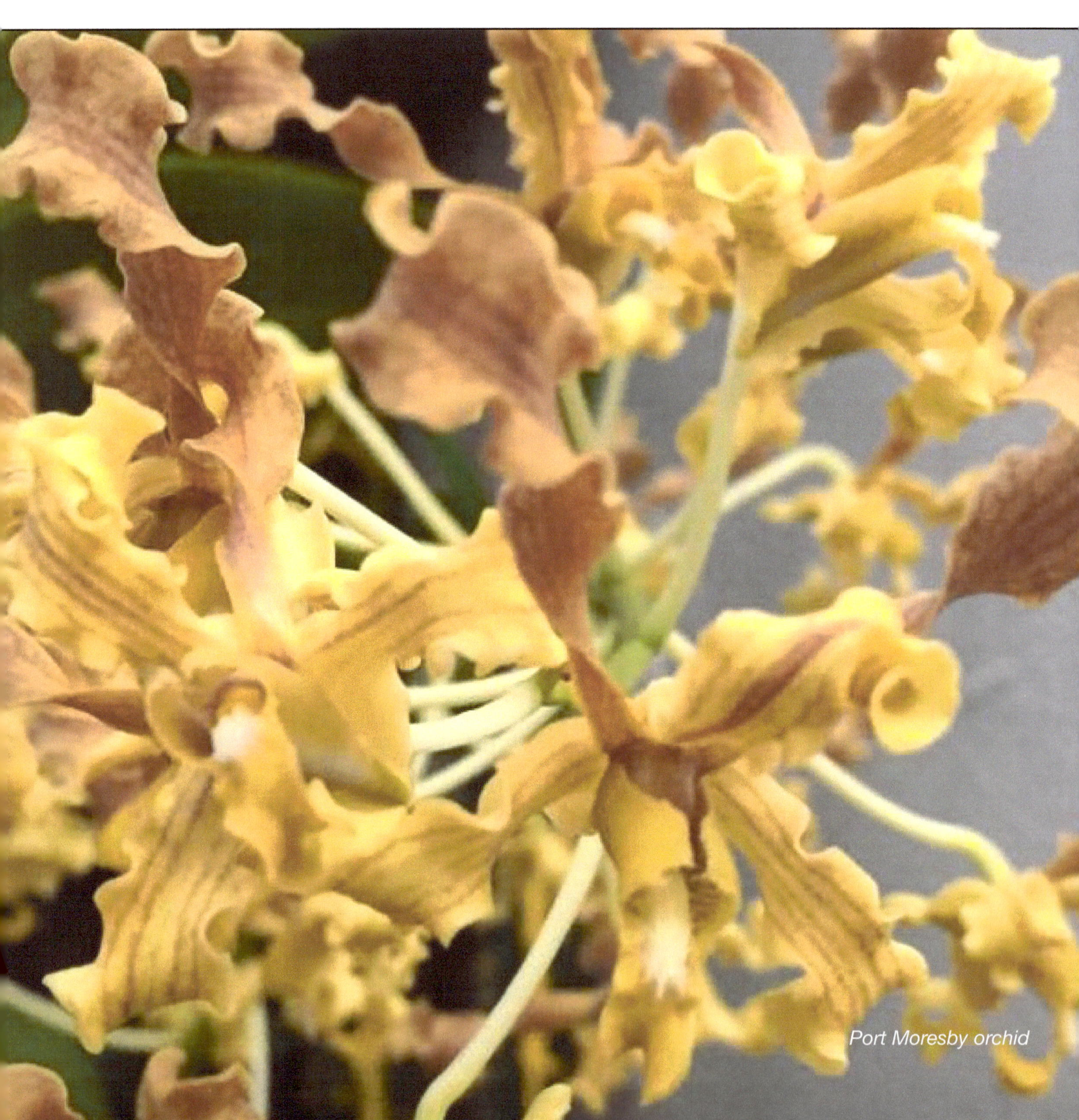
Port Moresby orchid

"A Manus Island refugee transferred to Papua New Guinea's Port Moresby for medical treatment says food rations refugees are selling to buy other essentials have been reduced. The refugee said the cut was a reaction to the men selling their milk for 30 US cents per bottle". RNZ news

MANUS ALERT   MAN ON MESSENGER

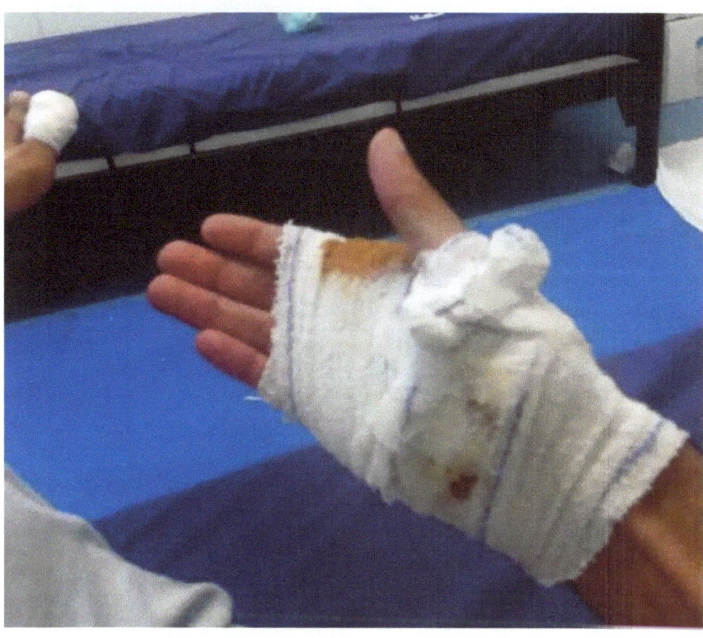

Refugee used mirror to deeply cut hand.
No facilities on Manus to treat mental illness.
IHMS made many people medication addicts then suddenly stopped medication & mental health treatment.

MAN: My roommate they invited for night out
But I'm really no desire
I think that I'm getting too old.

JILL: You must be joking old?

MAN: Really I have no desire to go nightclub.

JILL: Ok sleep well

MAN: Good night aunty.

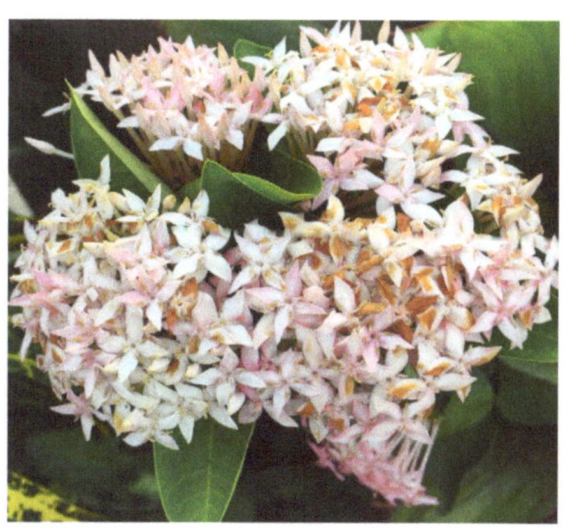

Flowers close to the hotel in Port Morsby.

I cannot contain my anger as I read of the juxtaposition of the cruelty which causes a man such depression that he cuts his wrist and the lack of medical support to treat his condition.
Man, I understand that you don't want to go to a nightclub with your mates but if you are too old at not quite thirty what am I at seventy?

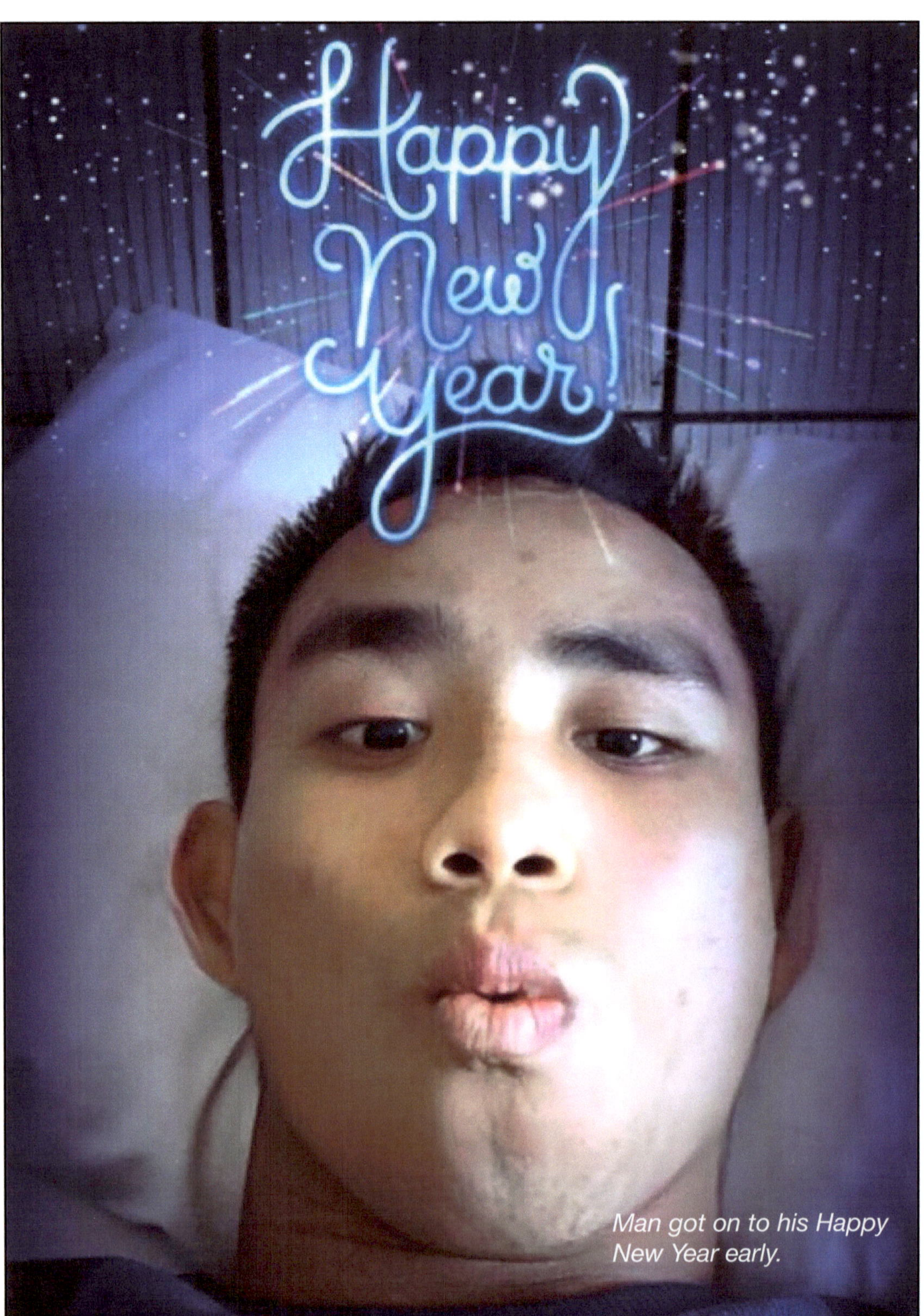

Man got on to his Happy New Year early.

> **"The Manus catastrophe has brought into focus Australian refugee brutality, and tens of thousands of people across Australia have protested. ... equality, now its time to say yes to refugees".**
> **Refugee Action Collective**

MANUS ALERT

MAN ON MESSENGER

Moz from #Manus on 3CR Australian community radio at 10 am tomorrow, 31 Dec 2017, New Years Eve. They will play " all the same."
We are ALL the same. Help us keep our SANITY. Remember our HUMANITY.

MAN: Good afternoon my aunty. Have a good day. Too early to say happy new year??

JILL: Never too early for that Man. May your new year be wonderful and filled with joy and new beginnings. Perhaps this will be the year we meet face to face.

MAN: Thanks I'm so hoping for meet you.

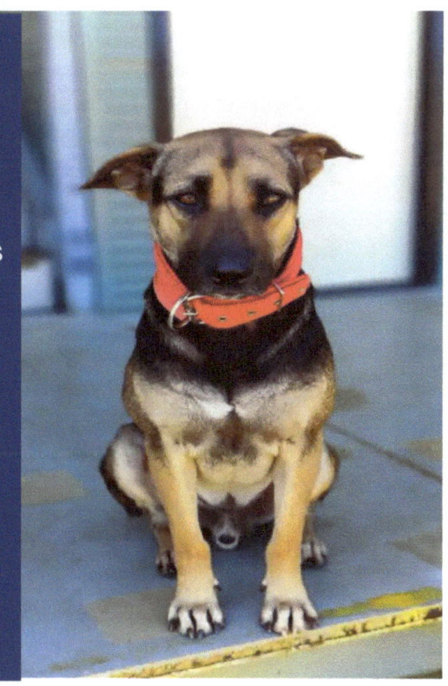

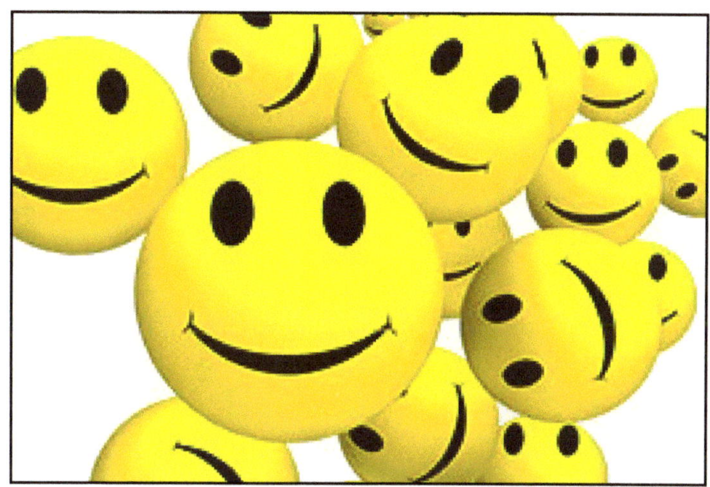

JILL: Me too.

Every now and then I am overcome by emotions good and bad, happy and sad. I so love all of you my Manus friends. Your compassion for each other is wonderful and Manus Alert, your turn- ing to Moz your dog, to express your distress is beautiful.

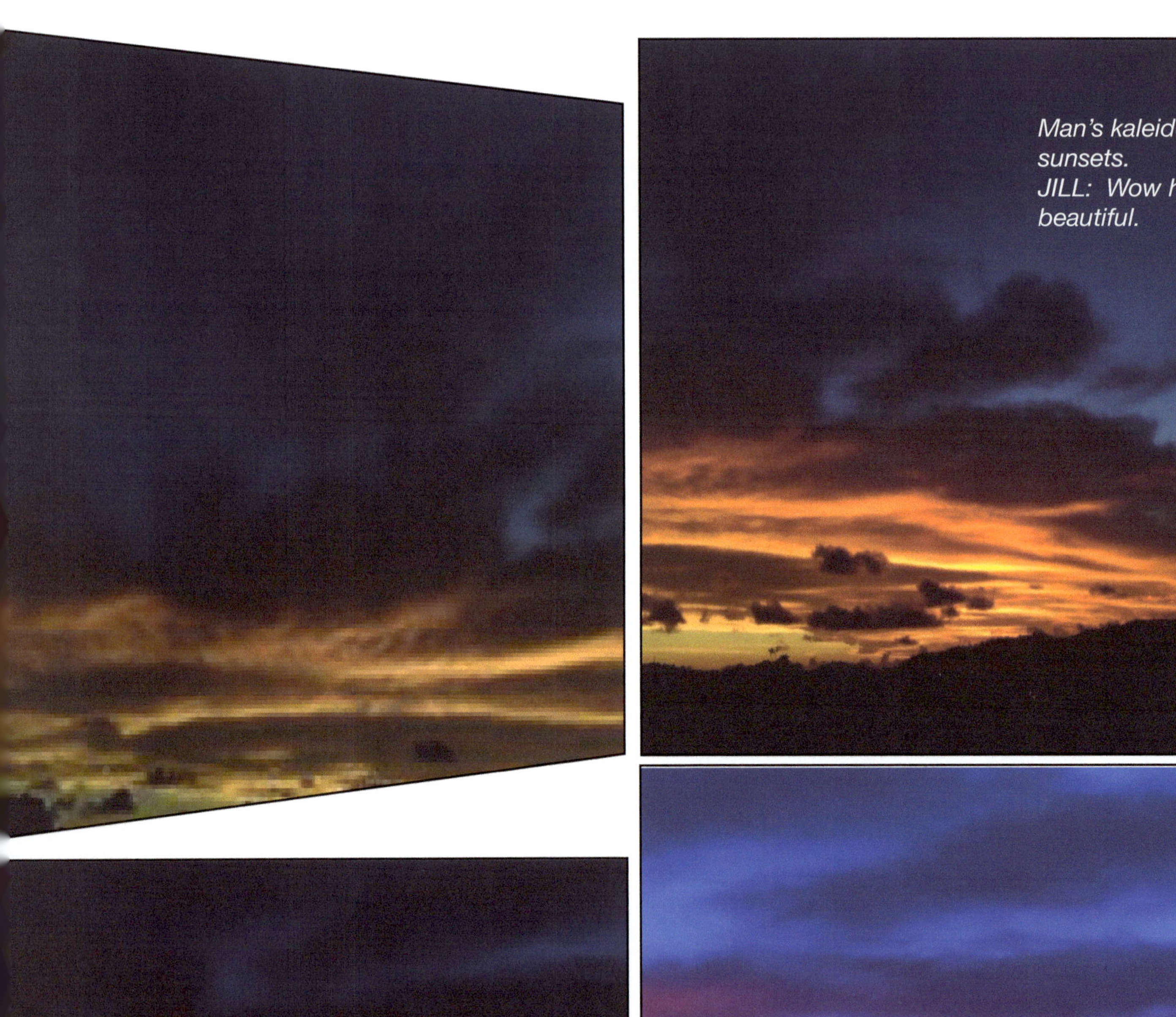
Man's kaleidoscope of
sunsets.
JILL: Wow how
beautiful.

<table>
<tr><td>

1

JAN

2018

</td><td>

"The Manus camp has been widely criticised since its 2012 reopening - just like Nauru. The United Nations and human rights groups have described conditions in the centres as horrid, saying that refugees living there are subject to 'severe abuse and neglect'". Al Jazeera

</td></tr>
</table>

MANUS ALERT

I (a manus refugee) want to share my feeling with lovely people of Australia.

I did not decide to flee my country and family but the war and situation force me to leave my country. I have known a humanitarian country called Australia which gave safety to oppressed and coerced people like me in past.

Not in my case Australian Government give me five and continue years of imprisonment for seeking asylum, unaccountable torture, suffering, wounds and cries, deaths of my friends.

I live a life where system kill my every day every hour every minutes while my same boat people released in Australian community since 2013. Two years before I got positive refugee status am still in detention.

I am begging for mercy. Let me and people like me on Manus, go.

MAN ON MESSENGER

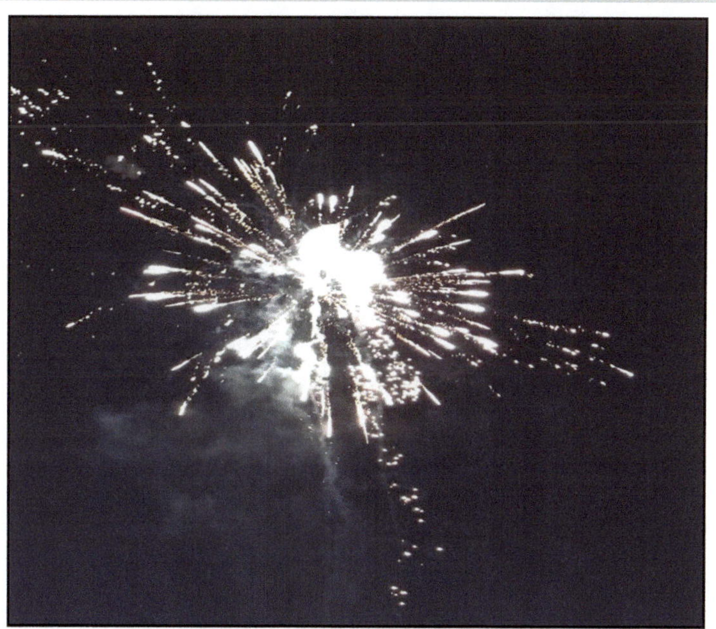

MAN: Thanks aunt

JILL: Lisa my daughter did the fireworks this year in a small country town.

MAN: Did you enjoy??

JILL: Very much. Now we have to drive 2 hours to get home. Just got home and put Mika to bed.

New year is a time to celebrate. Thank you Manus Alert for remembering that there are those among us who have some humanity and do not agree with the atrocities our government seems to enjoy.

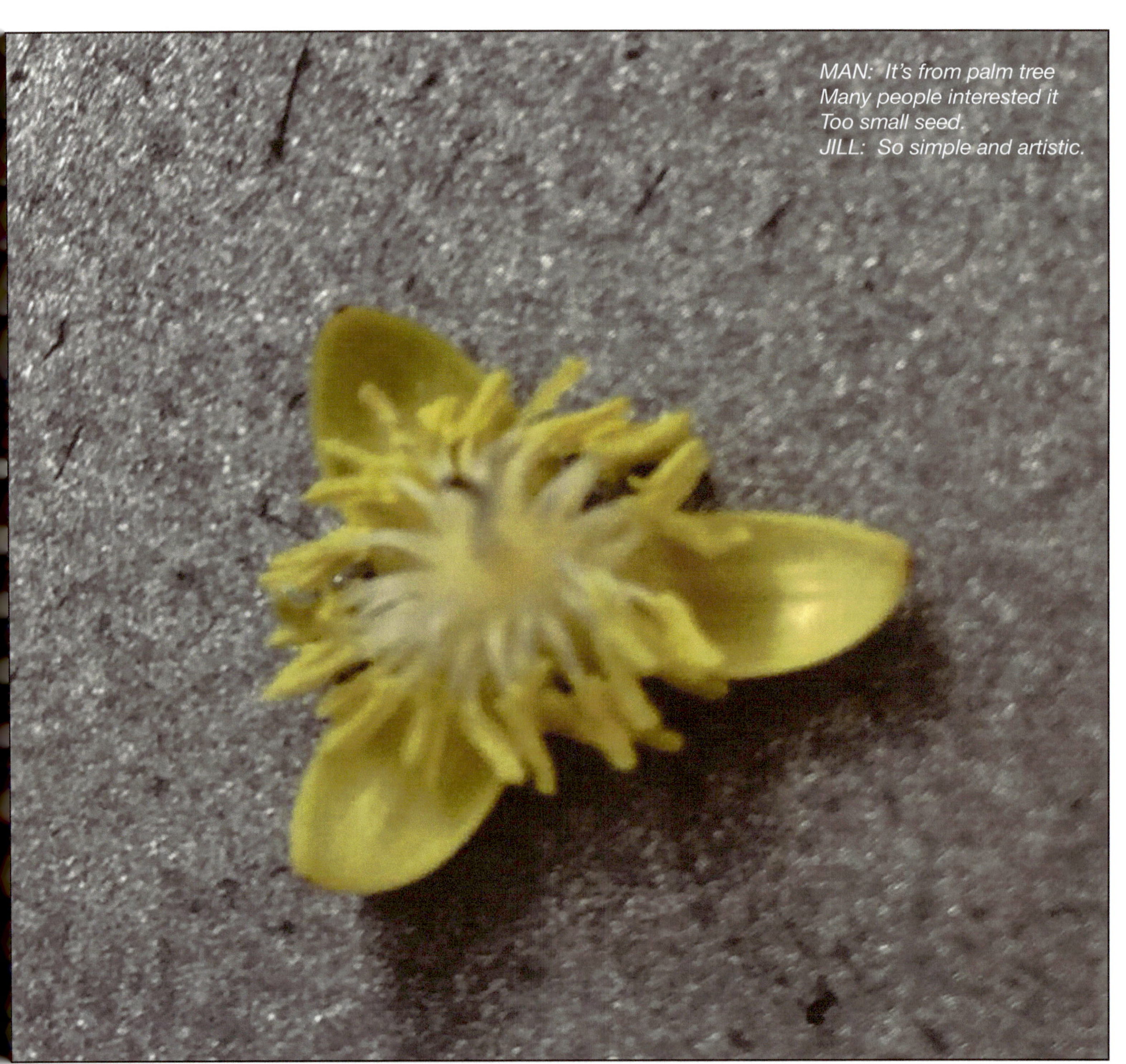
MAN: It's from palm tree
Many people interested it
Too small seed.
JILL: So simple and artistic.

<table>
<tr><td>

2 JAN 2018

</td><td>

Today the video of violent removals of detainees from Lombrum (November 24th November, 2017) was still prominent on many Facebook sites: "This morning in the RPC. Police and immigration are using violence again, for the 2nd day in a row, to force the men into the buses and to town". Gifts for Manus and Nauru - The Guardian.

</td></tr>
</table>

MANUS ALERT　　　　　　　**MAN ON MESSENGER**

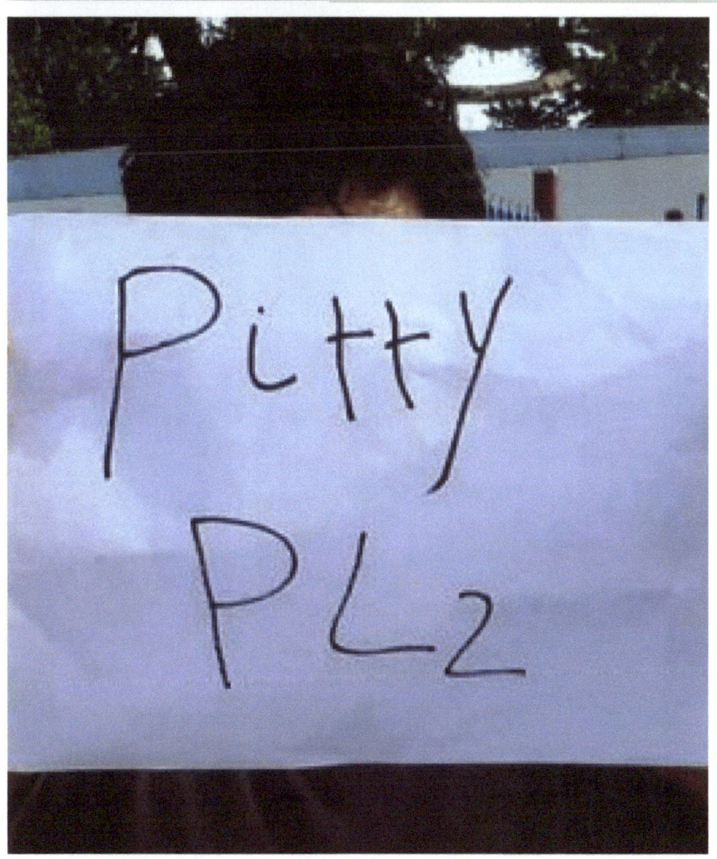

MAN: Sunday is great day of you because of church service and end of the 2017 . Good to pray for 2018.

JILL: I hope so my friend. You will be there with me.

MAN: I'll. We can go to the church one day.

JILL: For me church is not so important. It is my God that is and I can be with him anywhere. He exists beyond religion. And includes all.

MAN: Good aunty I do believe and agreed with you. Just most important is heart. We can practice our religion in anywhere and anytime. Places and timers are just a method.

JILL:Yes we are one in our beliefs.

MAN: Aunty. I'm going to my lunch now. Have a great day.

Man always has been and continues to be a peacemaker. Australia would have gained so much from him had we welcomed his arrival. I agree that every country has the right to manage their borders but to punish people for seeking asylum while being signatories to a convention which supports the rights of asylum seekers to reach out for assistance is wrong.

RPC = Regional Processing Centre

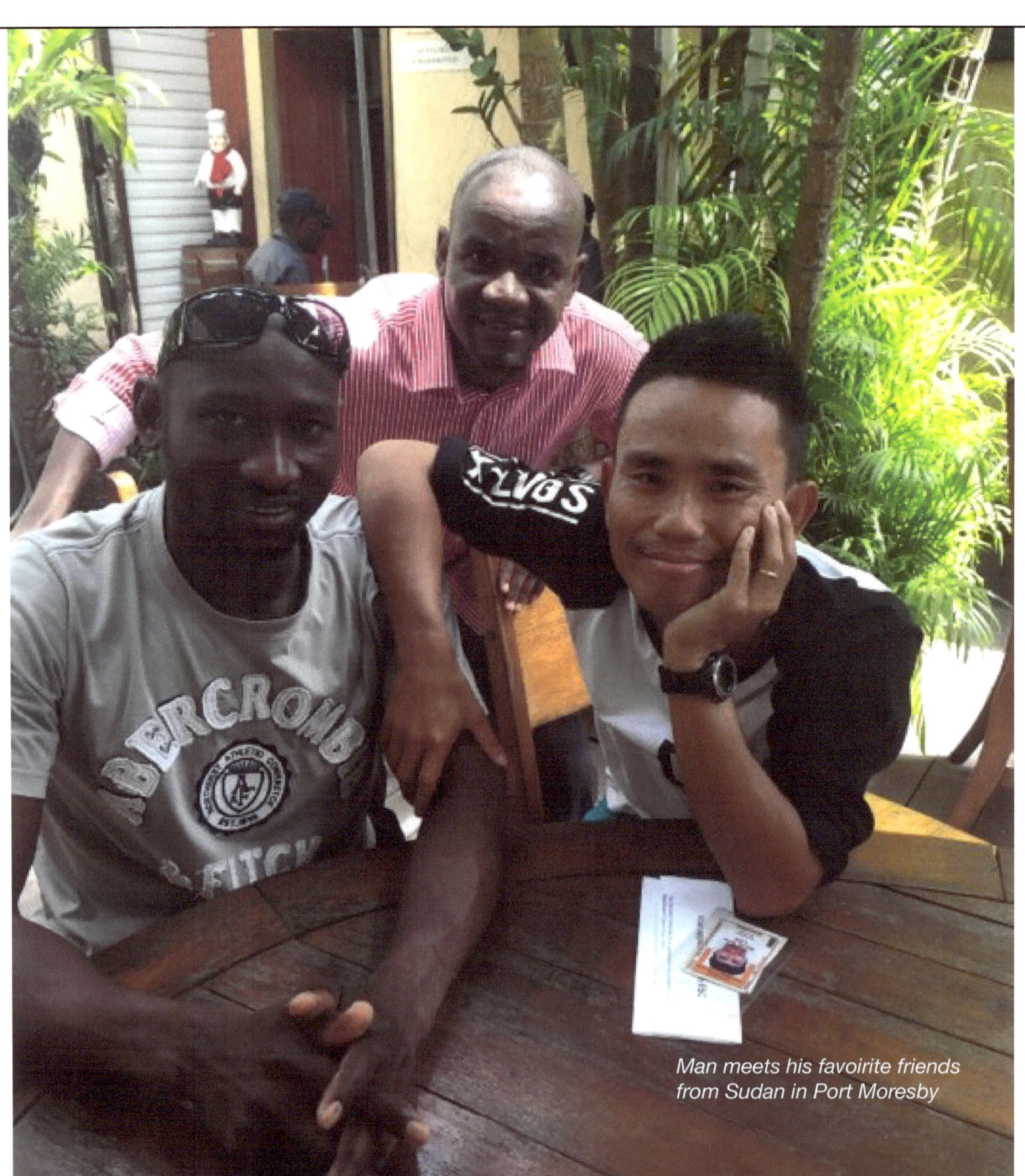

Man meets his favoirite friends from Sudan in Port Moresby

"Help Us!" The government's cruelty has cut the refugees off from the countries of their birth but left them unable to reach the countries of their dreams. In terms of physical suffering, fear and desperation, there was no comparison. Manus is a purgatory – made in Australia".
Tim Costello

MANUS ALERT   MAN ON MESSENGER

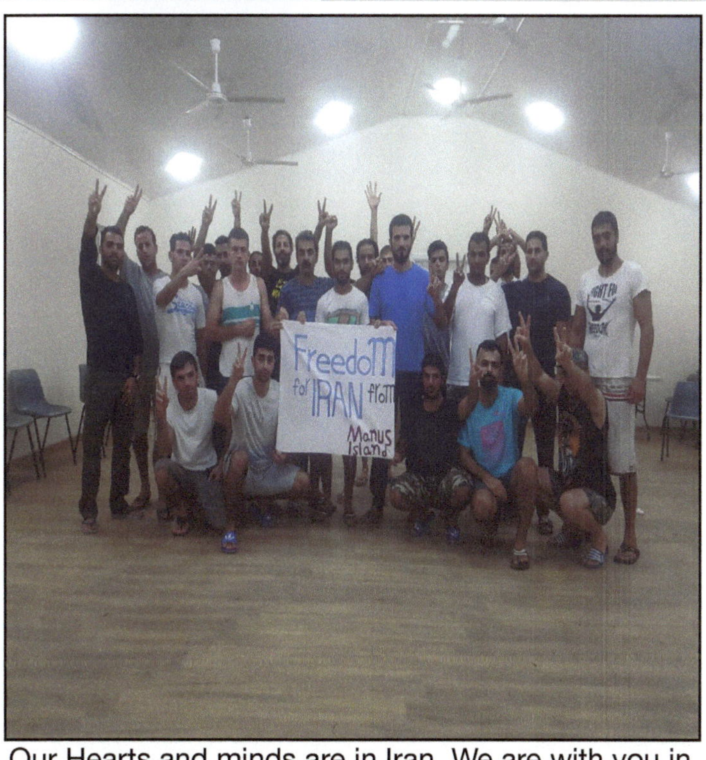

Our Hearts and minds are in Iran. We are with you in heart and Wish Freedom For Iran.
Manus Island

MAN: Aunty I saw your post it's about a Sudanese. Did he help you ??

JILL: Yes exactly as I said.

MAN: Yes. I love them I more closed with them in Manus. They are very friendly And frankly.. really I did enjoy with them so much.

JILL: This young man was beautiful and gentle.

MAN: There are Sudanese. We met again in here. They are waiting for going back home.

JILL: That is sad.

MAN: Sad for them. Very sad. I was more closing with Somalian and Sudanese. They have no pretending much.

JILL: Just generous. Both good peoples from my Africa.

I quote Tim Costello because his words say it so clearly. "My first glimpse of Manus refugees was of desperate faces shouting "Help us" as Papua New Guinea police, doing the Australian government's dirty work, broke up the former detention centre. They forcibly removed more than 300 men who were refusing to go to the new facilities, 24km away, in no small part because it offered no solution to their indefinite detention."

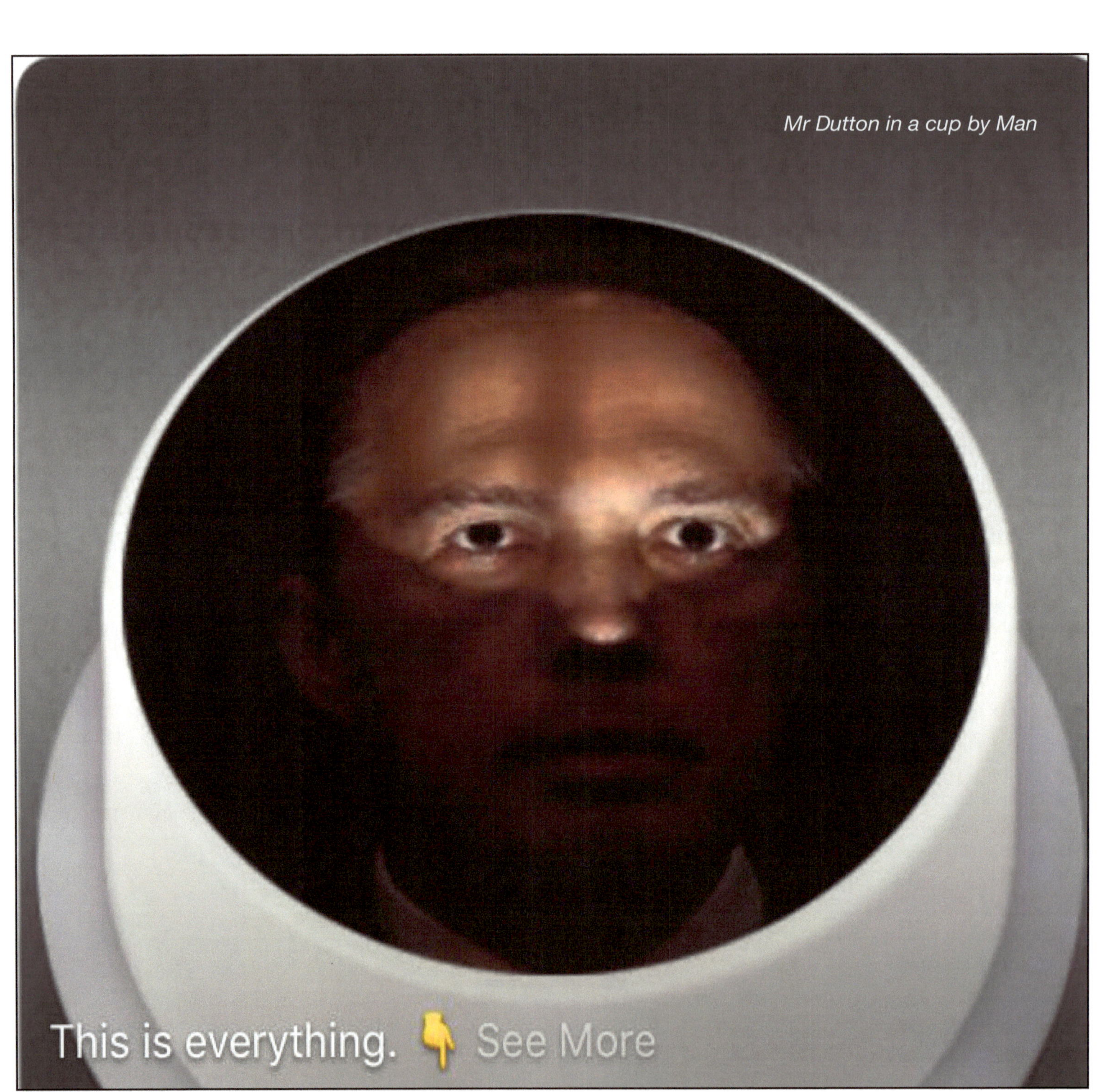
Mr Dutton in a cup by Man
This is everything. 👇 See More

"The Refugee Action Collective (Vic) held a vigil for Faysal Ahmet today. Faysal was born 20 June 1989 and died 24 December 2016. He was 27 years ld and in the care of the Australian Government". Facebook

MANUS ALERT

MAN ON MESSENGER

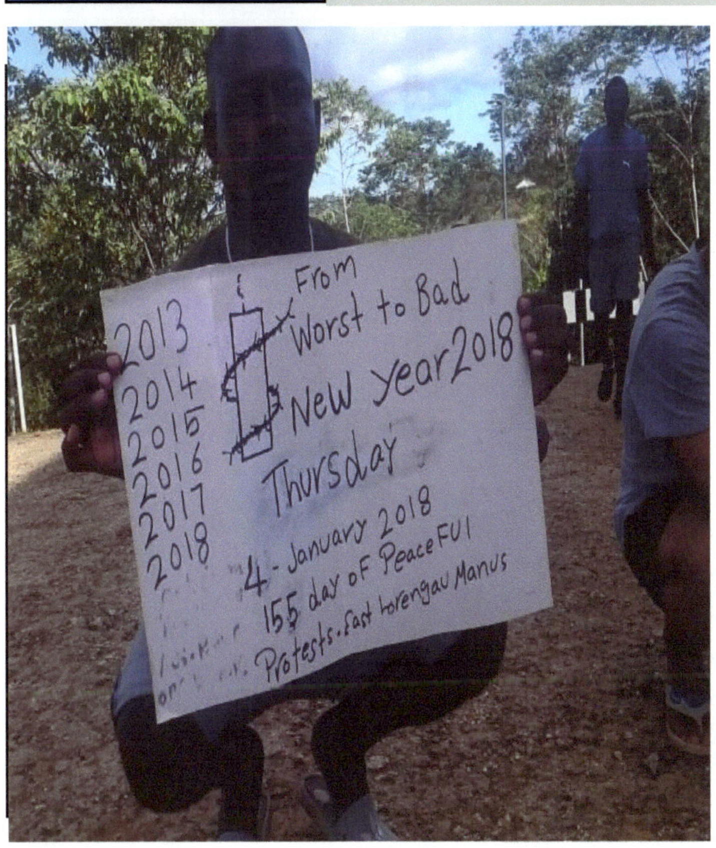

MAN: Hi aunt when I have been out of from this country and Dutton's hand I would like to give a crocheted beanie to Dutton..Who can hand over him and is it good idea??

JILL: I am happy to send it to him for you.

MAN: At least we can show refugees behaviors

JILL: You can actually send it yourself if you like with a letter telling him what you would like him to know. The only difference if I do it for you is that I can check if he gets it.

MAN: I think that if you helped me it's better.

JILL: Sure just send it to me with a note or send it and message me what you want to say.

MAN: I want to know he received my beanie or not. Then I'll post a letter to you for him when I arrived in USA

JILL: OK just send it to me and I will post it.

MAN: Thanks.

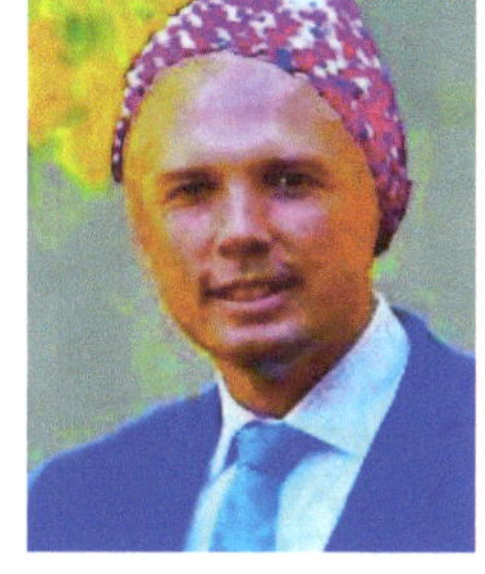

Artwork by David Parris

Man makes me smile. I cannot imagine what Dutton would do with a beanie but I do know that he and his colleagues can learn much from my compassionate friend. Go Man.

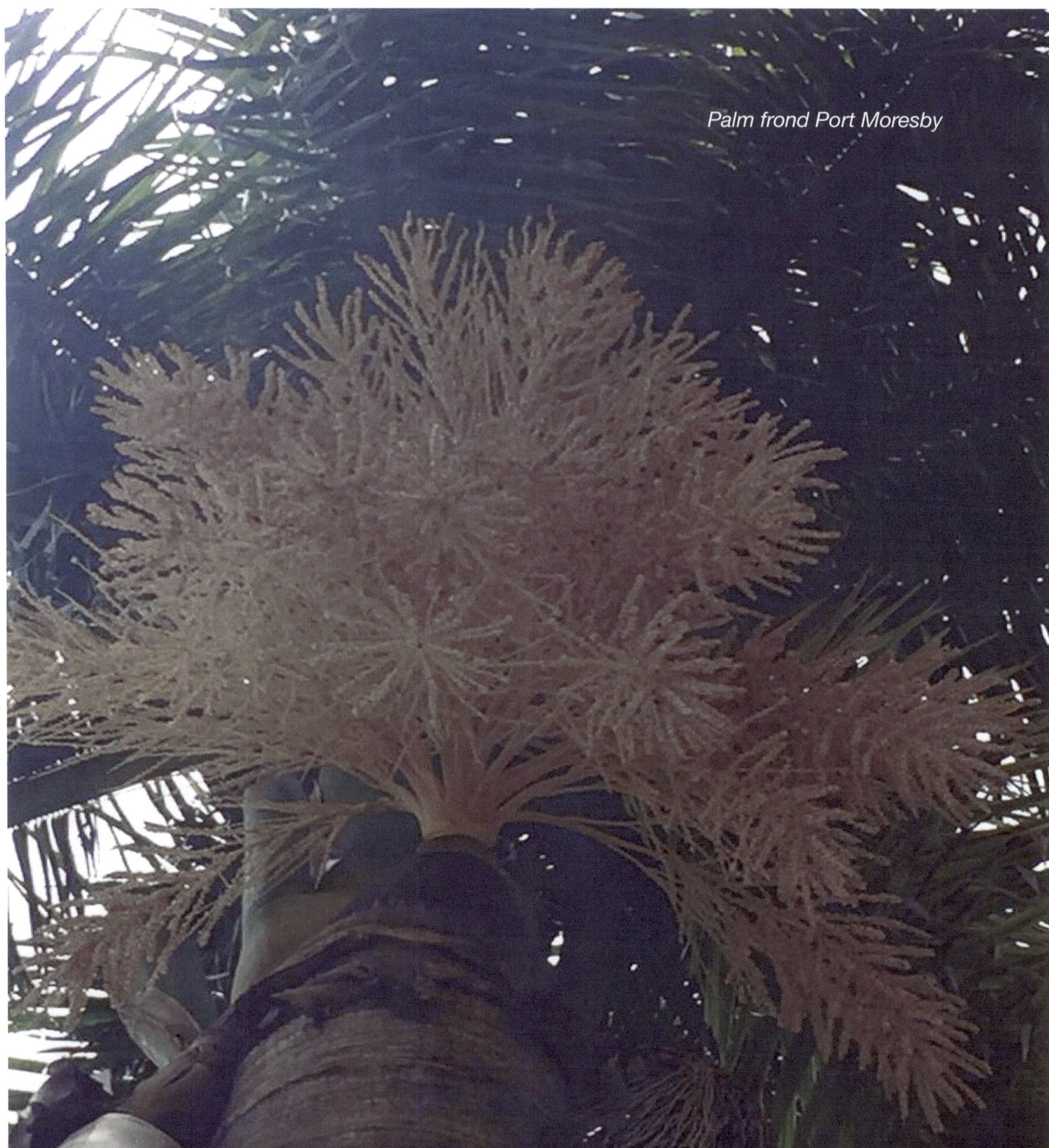
Palm frond Port Moresby

"AMA president, Dr Gannon said he told Minister Dutton that the AMA would remain a strong advocate for asylum seekers, and call out any injustices or any weakening of Australia's human rights obligations but failed. We are ashamed". Sister Jane Irene Keogh

MANUS ALERT   MAN ON MESSENGER

MAN: I have an appointment for cultural class. Now I'm waiting my medical checkup appointment and I know my departure date. 23th January.

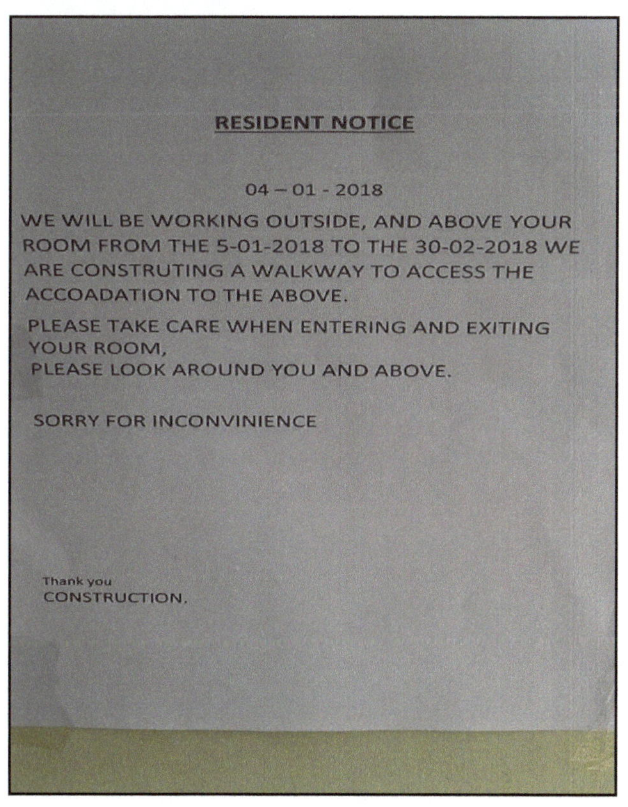

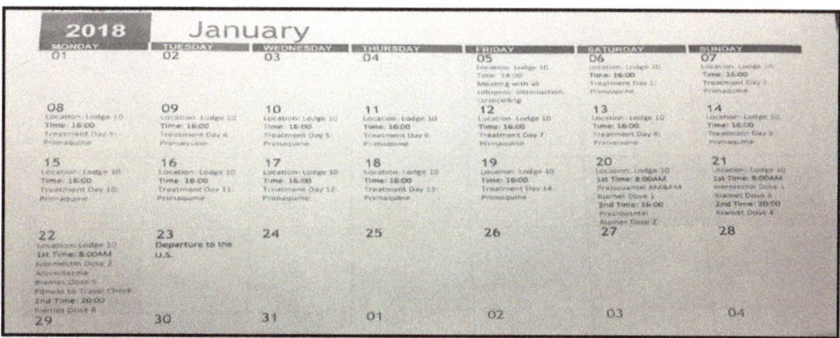

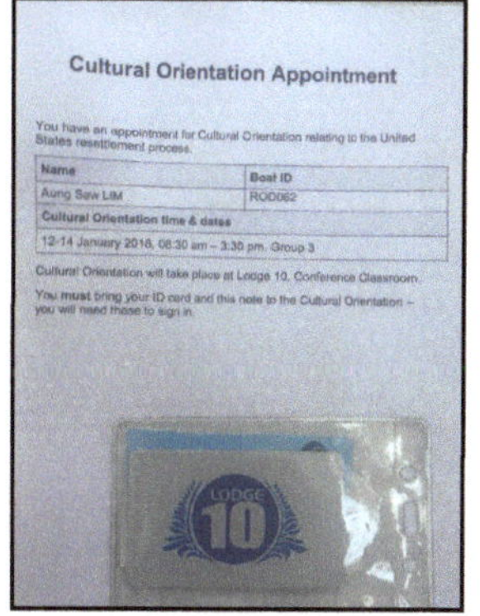

MAN: Aunty we have to take the medication for two weeks.

JILL: Yes so you don't take PNG diseases to the US.

MAN: Anyway I always knew my departure date. And also we don't know yet our town in USA .

"AMA President Michael Gannon has failed in his attempt to get Health Minister Peter Dutton to agree to the AMA's offer to send a group of independent medical experts to assess the psychological and physical health of the hundreds of men on Manus Island". I guess this means that Dutton does not want the health of detainees monitored or treated.
I am pleased that the Americans take the health of those going to the USA more seriously but must question why the detainees have not been treated prophylactically as an integral part of Australia's duty of care.

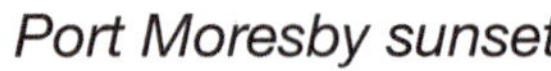
Port Moresby sunset

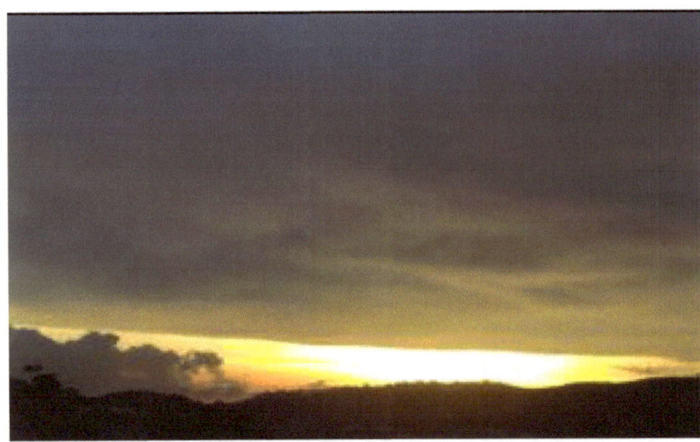

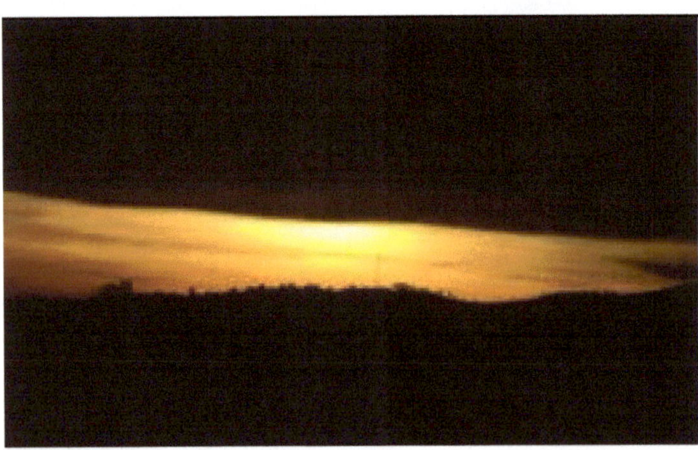

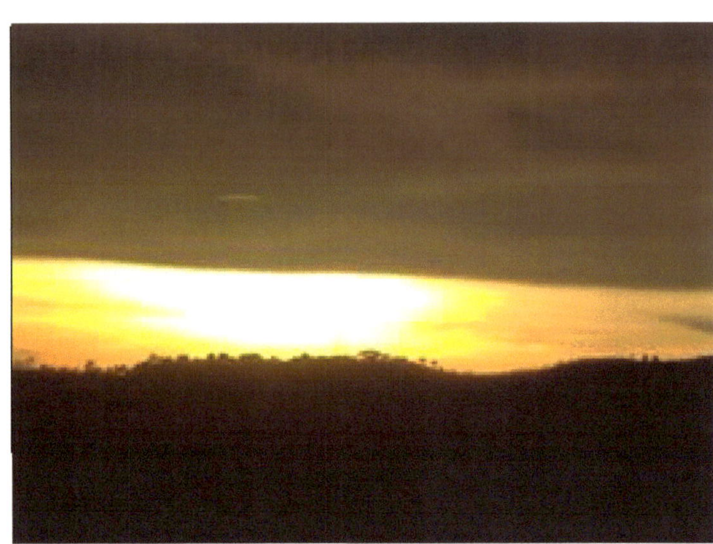

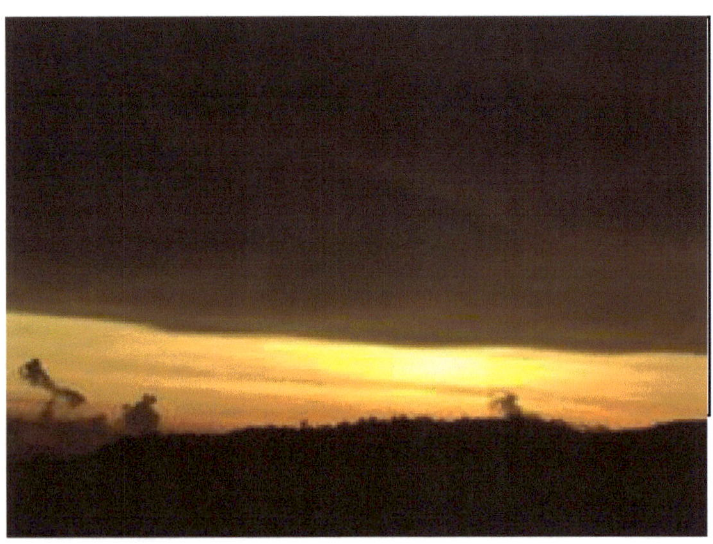

"When I meet these men and when I speak with them, I see people who are not just victims of mistreatment by Australia, but tremendous lost opportunities for Australia. Today marks 1625 days for many off shore detainees".
Daniel Webb Human Rights Law Centre

MANUS ALERT   MAN ON MESSENGER

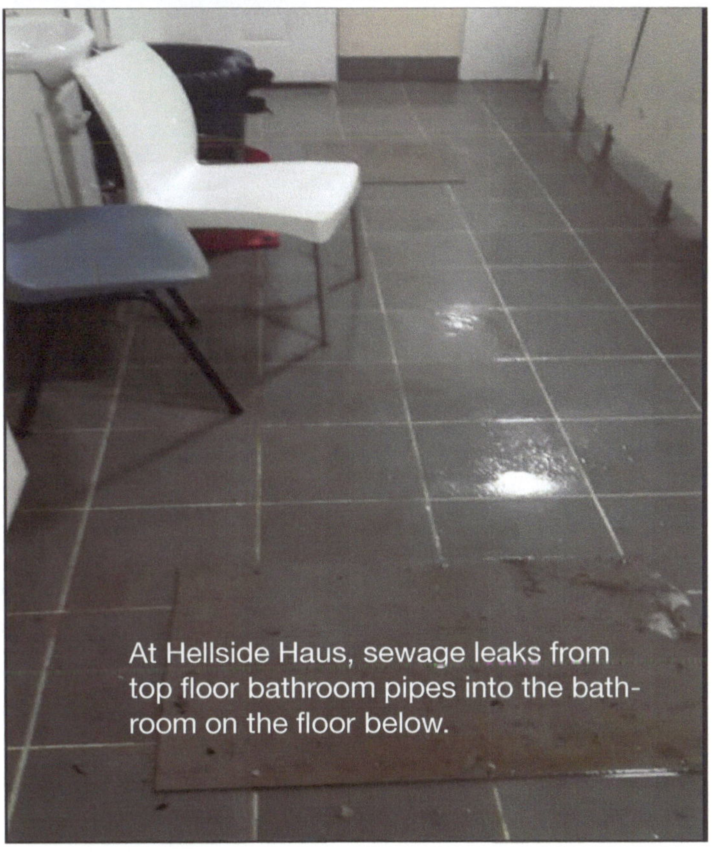
At Hellside Haus, sewage leaks from top floor bathroom pipes into the bathroom on the floor below.

MAN: Hi aunty. Please could you let me know when the museum will be displaying my crafts ? Then if you go there again could you take the picture of their display.. ,? I would love to see and learn how they are displaying to my crafts . My ex case manager also wants to visit and look. She is living in Melbourne. She is my crafts teacher and an advocator.

Her name is XXX and I had have mention her many times.

Thanks my aunty.

JILL: I will ask the Immigration Museum to let me know as soon as the exhibition is organised. I know it takes quite a while. In the meantime if you want me to send a book to XXX let me know her name and address.

I am so pleased to be a part of facilitating the conservation and display of Man's work. It would be an immense shame to allow the history of men like Man to be forgotten.
I am aware that it is very important to Man that his lost time gains some meaning and recognition. His young life was sacrificed to Manus. To have this acknowledged goes some way towards recognising stolen years.
I love that Man pursues this process and holds me accountable for making it happen.

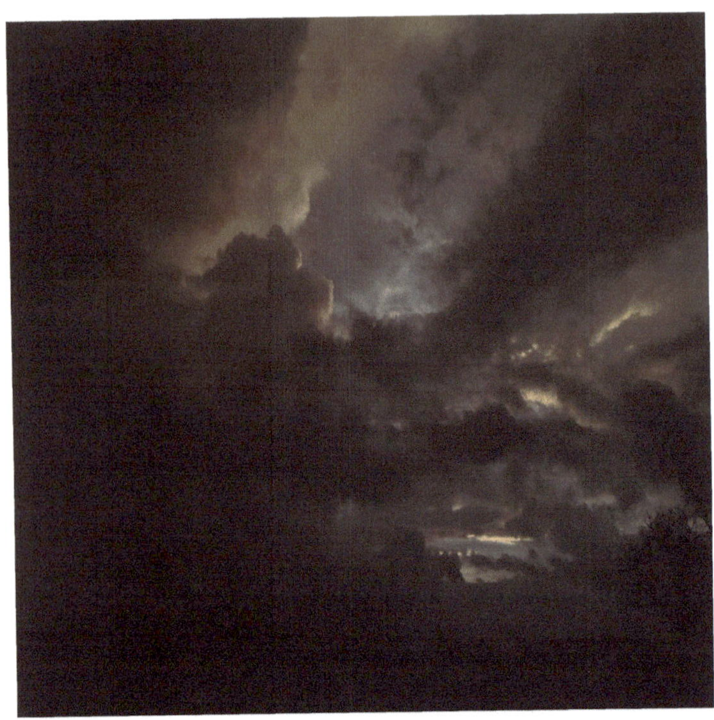

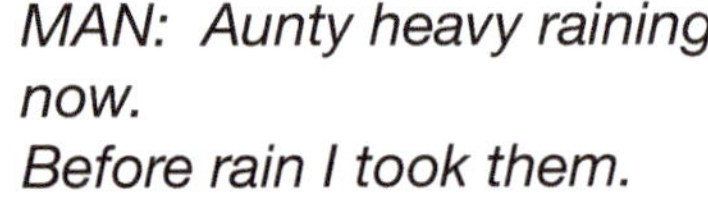

MAN: Aunty heavy raining
now.
Before rain I took them.

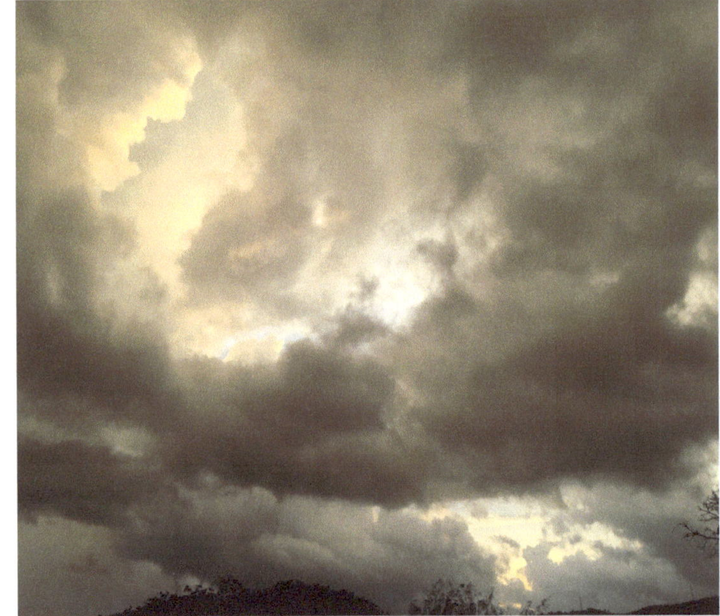

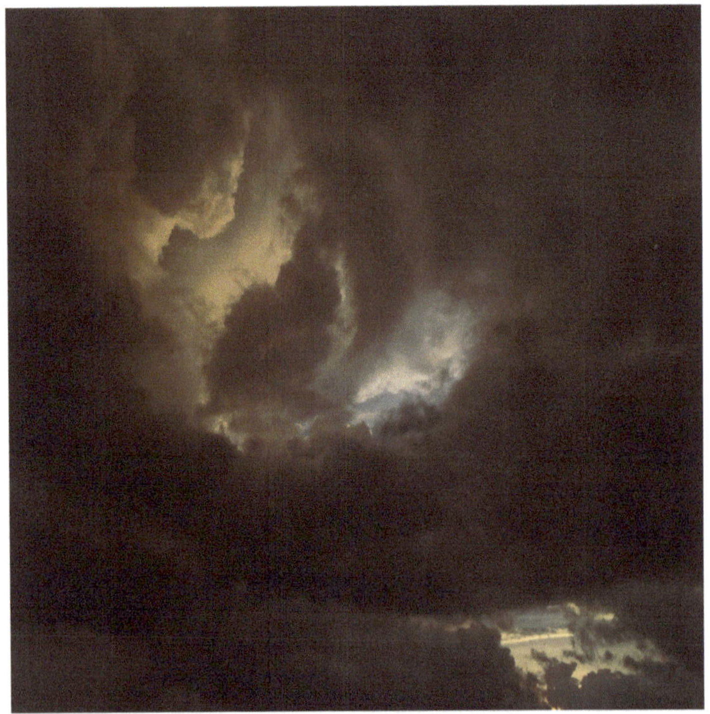

"Figures released earlier this year showed the federal government has spent $5 billion on offshore immigration detention since 2012. Australia has spent more than $1 million for each of the 2,000 people who have been detained at the detention centre on Manus".
Jenny Hayward-Jones RAC

MANUS ALERT   MAN ON MESSENGER

Kicked
Sunday
7 January 2018
158th day of peaceful protests
West Waste Haus Manus

A man was kicked by a guard.

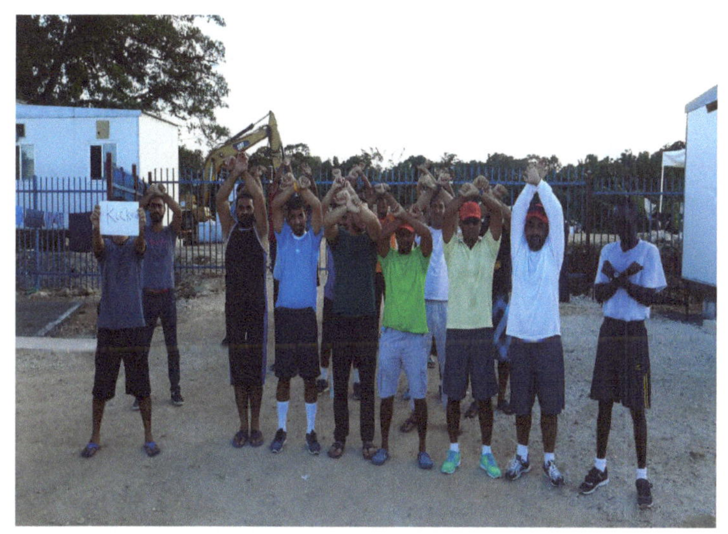

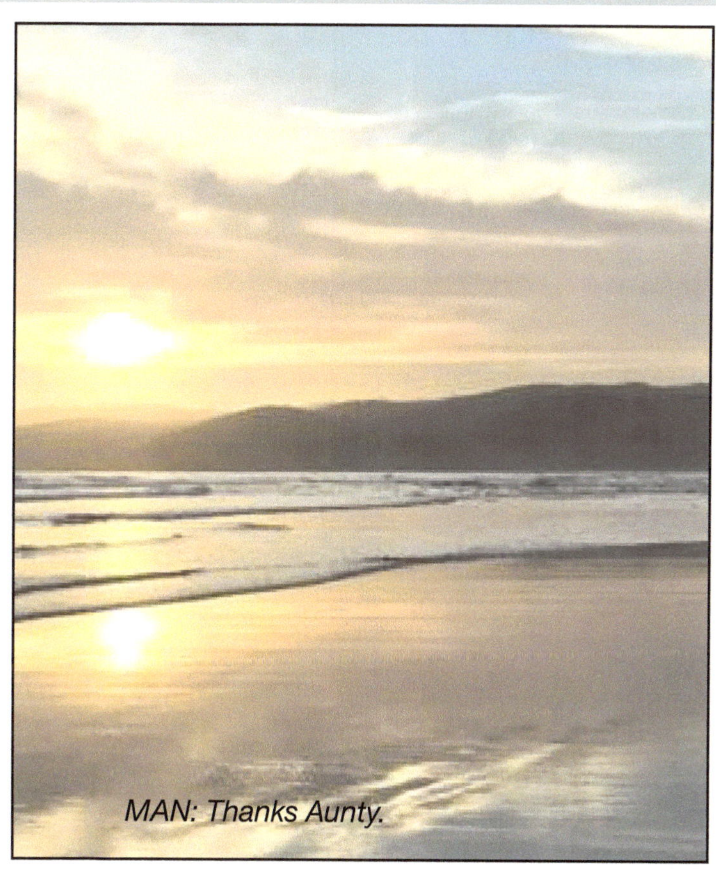

MAN: Thanks Aunty.

What happens on Manus goes beyond mismanagement. Men are hurt and no one is held responsible. In the light of this continual onslaught it is amazing that the detainees maintain their peaceful demonstrations. If only Australia would stop for just a moment and recognise what they could learn from those they persecute.

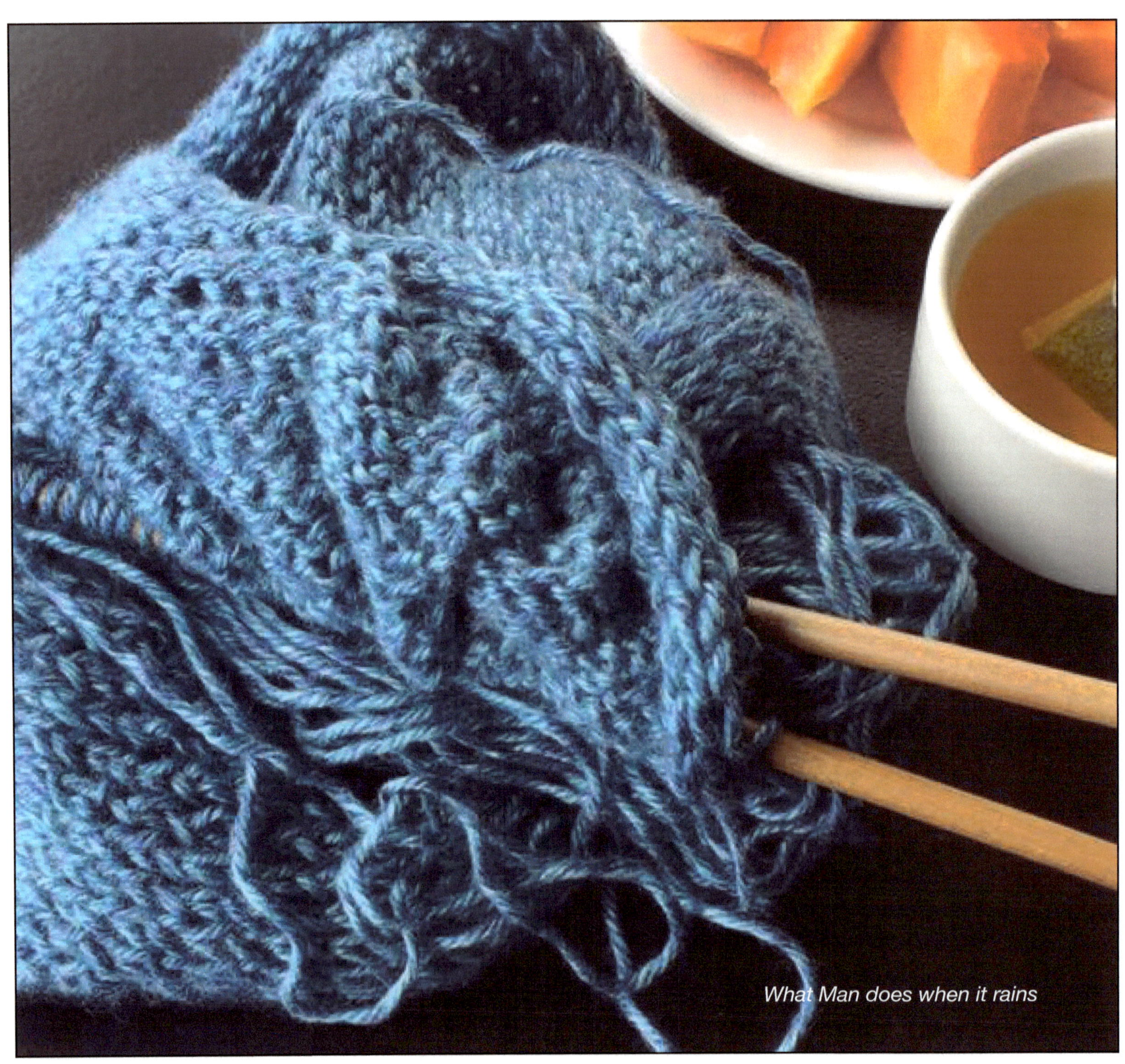
What Man does when it rains

"The compensation offered to detainees on Manus was $45,000. Many men left their aged parents or their children without a bread winner for five years. Many carry illnesses now that will need serious treatment. Building a new life in the US, if they are granted asylum, will cost over twice that". Marilyn Beech (government made a $70,000,000 out of court settlement to stop case going to court.)

MANUS ALERT   **MAN ON MESSENGER**

Manus refugees forced to sell their food.

108 Manus refugees were transferred to Port Moresby for medical treatment & are lodged in the Granville Motel. They are given three meals a day but no allowance for other necessities. The refugees sell their lunch for five kina, about $2 Australian, so they can buy toiletries like soap & shampoo.

MAN: Morning aunt

JILL: Hi you should be asleep

Yes but my stomach is unwell and also Feeling sad. A little bit.

JILL: Oh because you leaving?
Malaria medication can make you feel unwell

MAN: Yes. I'm sad because I could not meet with my friends including you . Actually USA is too far with you guys

JILL: Yes it is far and it will be very different.

MAN: Please try to get sleep aunty too late for you as well.

JILL: Yes but I had a long afternoon nap and I am on my way to bed now

MAN: Bye aunty

Simply following the day to day happenings on Manus is horrific but perhaps the biggest indictment of these detention centres comes to mind in the turgid boredom I struggle with as I write my daily commentary. If this is so hard for me what must it be like for those who have lived for years in detention.

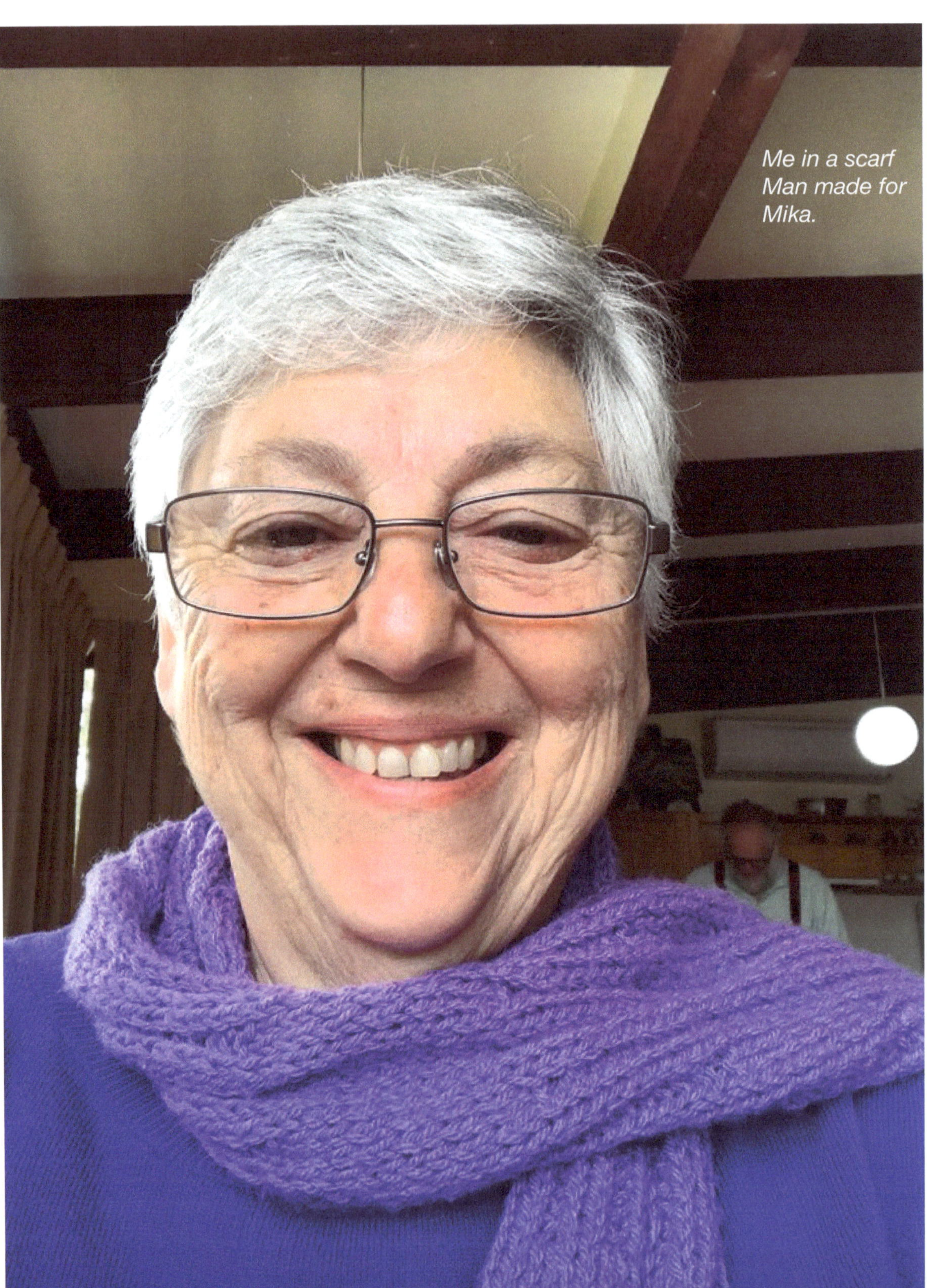
Me in a scarf
Man made for
Mika.

**"Australian citizens wrongfully detained because of immigration failures, report finds.
Poorly trained officers took no responsibility for flawed decisions that landed two Australians in immigration detention, despite being citizens".The Guardian**

MANUS ALERT   MAN ON MESSENGER

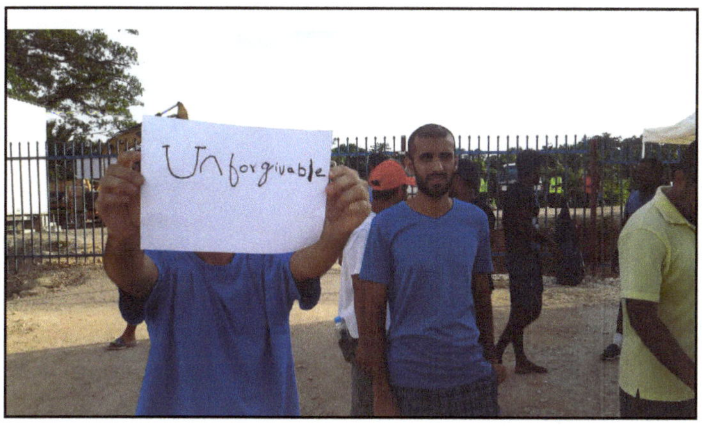

Tuesday
9 January 2018
160th day of peaceful protests
East Lorengau Manus
The sake of our peaceful protest is just for real freedom.

MAN: Maybe I got mental health problems because I don't want to talk in phone more than two minutes. I went to vision city with two roommates but shopped myself when we arrive to mall.
JILL: Adjustment problems that will pass or perhaps you are simply a loner. I have borrowed Mika's scarf.
                              Thank you. See the pic.
MAN: Lovely color aunty
I think that malaria pill is makes me feeling tired because I had ever medication .But I'm resting

MAN: Puzzle !!! What is it ??
If your answer is collected I'll kiss you.

JILL: White chilli?

MAN: No. Sorry you are my deserve with my kisses.

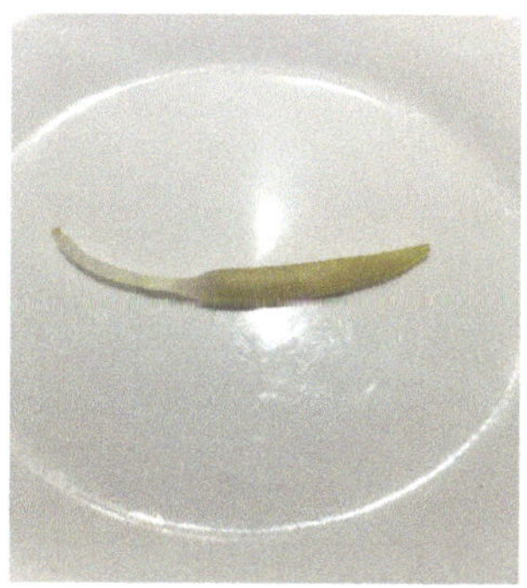

What a breath of fresh air. I love puzzles Man.
As for the powers of our Immigration department. This has happened before with Pauline Row.
Scary stuff could it be you or me next?

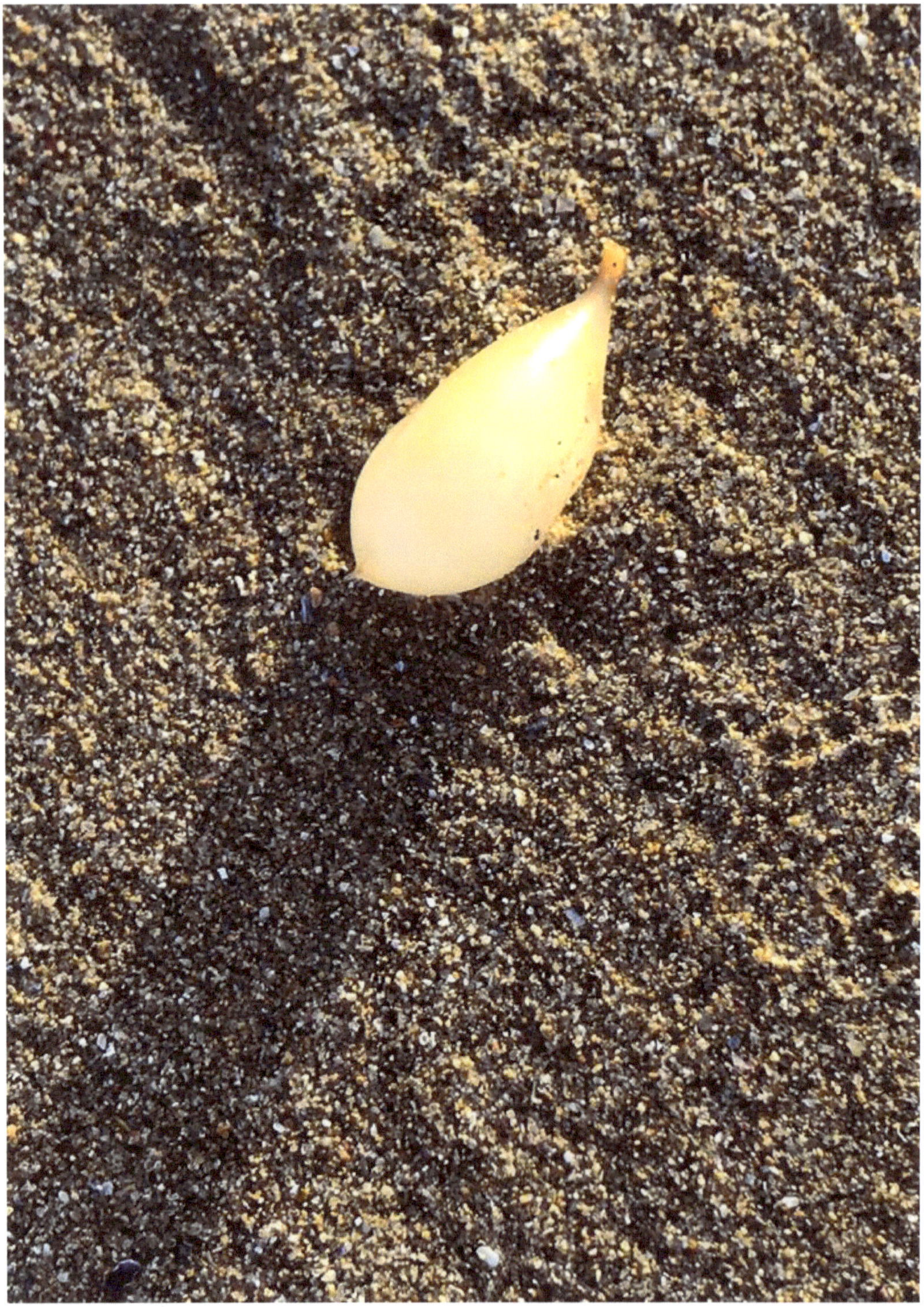

MAN: It's look like an onion?

JILL: Not an onion.

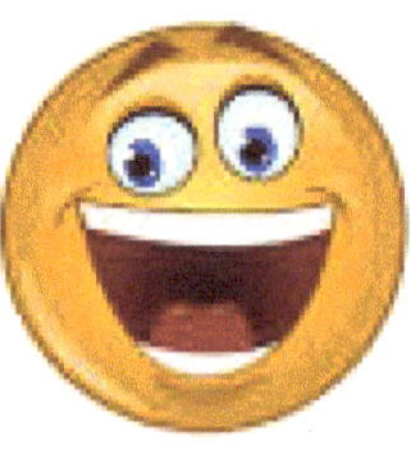

"A refugee in Port Moresby hospital has been on hunger strike for 20 days. He has high blood pressure and diabetes and the doctors have forced him to eat by getting authority from the court. Behrouz Boochani".   RNZ

MANUS ALERT

A Manus Island refugee transferred to Papua New Guinea's Port Moresby for medical treatment says food rations refugees are selling to buy other essentials have been reduced.

108 men from Manus are in the capital's Granville Motel and don't receive a weekly $US30 dollar allowance that's given to about 70 refugees in two other lodges in the city.

The refugees in Granville sell their lunches and beverages in order to afford toiletries that are not supplied.

On Monday night, the men were told their daily milk ration was cut from two 250 mililitre bottles to one.

The refugee said the cut was a reaction to the men selling their milk for 30 US cents per bottle.

He says their daily drinking-water ration has also been capped at six 600 millilitre bottles per man, which was previously unlimited.

The refugee said they were not selling the water but could earn about 75 US cents by selling 24 empty bottles.

(sometimes Manus Alert reposts to remind us that issues are ongoing)

MAN ON MESSENGER

MAN: Im listening a Burmese music. I listened to that music in 2013 hunger strike time. I had no food to eat so I just listened the music . Especially to this song.

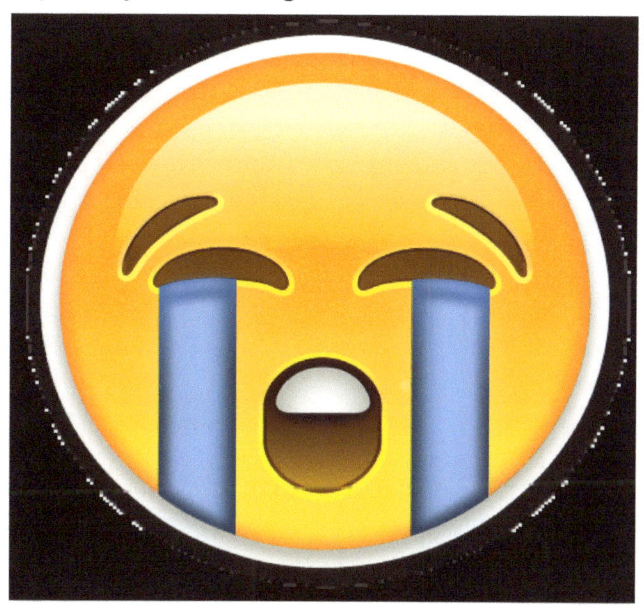

JILL: Does the music bring back sadness?

Wonderful emotions again. Man is allowing himself to grieve. This is so healthy.

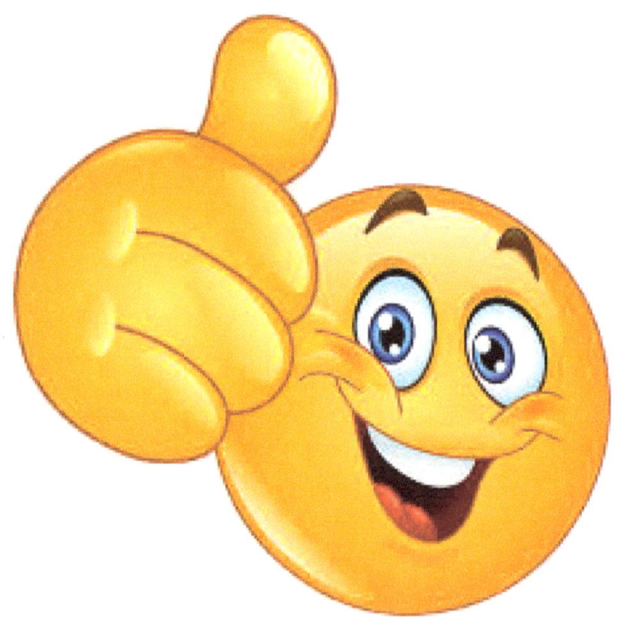

Man often gives me the thumbs
up as a thank you.

"Shorten urges Australia to accept New Zealand's Manus refugees offer despite rejecting the offer when in government. Federal Labor says Australia should consider New Zealand's ongoing offer to accept refugees from Manus Island". SBS Wires

MANUS ALERT

MAN ON MESSENGER

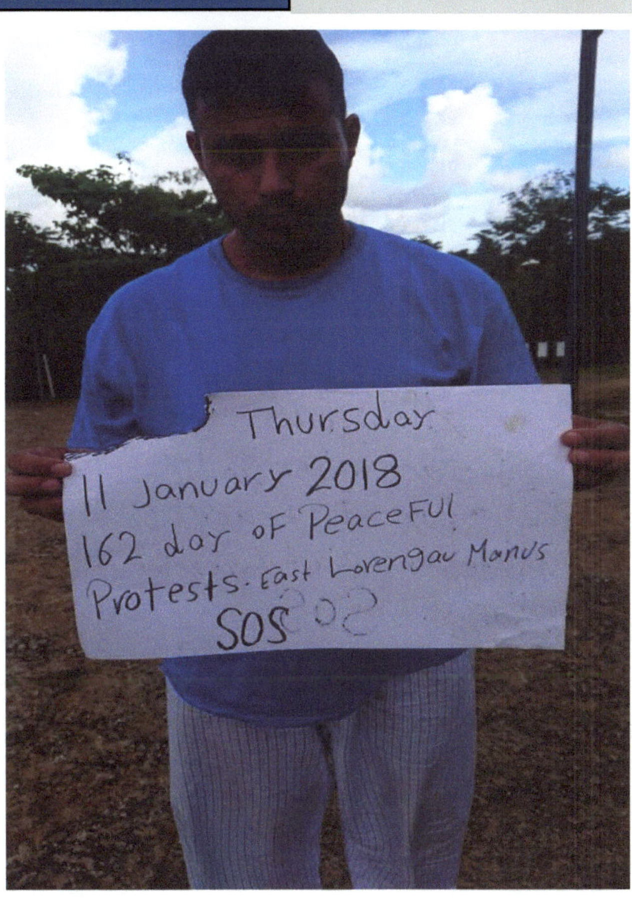

JILL: Hi Man I have texted with Jane who wants you to do some stuff for her is it OK to speak to her?

MAN: Ok I'm happy aunt. Even I'm no more involved with Oz but a lot of my friends are still in there. No hiding any more. Time to say all trusts.

JILL: OK I will tell Jane but she will need to get written permission from you unless you want to give me written permission to do everything in Australia for you.

MAN: Please let me know If someone wants to talk about PNG people. How they threaten us. I'll share my experiences with png people.

JILL: Not sure what you mean Man are you saying you want to talk about the PNG People. If so please tell me.

MAN: PNG people discriminate against us.

JILL: Are they treating you badly?

MAN: Of course. That's why I'll share to Oz people what i got. Especially sexual harassment

JILL: OK I am very interested to hear and to support. If you want me to talk to people let me know how and I will make sure it is shared with newspapers and politicians like Nick McKim

What is wrong with New Zealand. Clearly torture is your preferred option Dutton. I am sick of excuses where is your humanity?
Another museum Man, and this time the National Museum Canberra, this is wonderful. We will remember you and so will our children and theirs.

Another sunset

A refugee with a serious mental illness is in Lorengau hospital. This man has become mentally unwell in the past few days. There are no psychological facilities in Manus to protect him.

Despite international condemnation,our future remains uncertain.The refugees are victims of Australian govt policies targeting asylum seekers who trying to seek their protection to indefinite detention.The worst part of it we re experiencing people bad mental illness without drugs.
Abdul Aziz Adam

An arrow can be only be shot by pulling it backward. When life gets set dragging you back with difficulties, just imagine that it is going to launch you into something great.

Day 163 peaceful protest. We won't give up until we get our freedom. We hope we will end up in a great life. (Shamindan Kanapadhi)

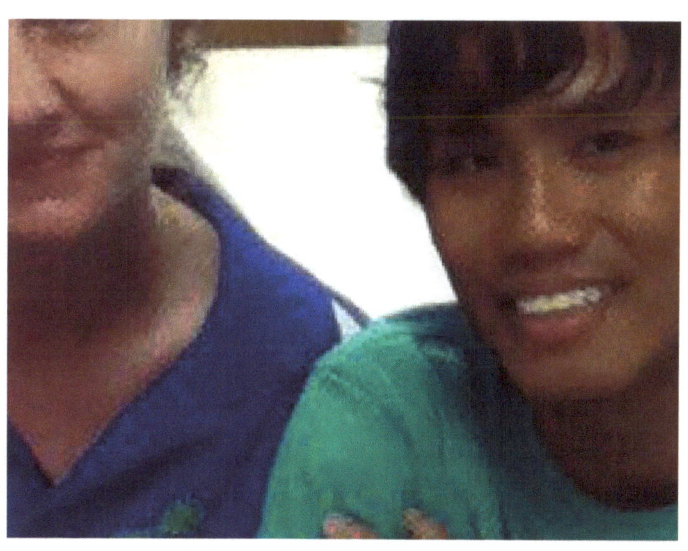

MAN: She one of the kindest lady from manus. She is from Recreation team. She was my oasis as well. She cried more then ten times in her routine for three weeks. Because of Wilson reports.

JILL: Sounds like a wonderful lady love her eyes and smile.

(I believe workers were not allowed to report what was happeningin writing.)

Again you reminisce Man. I love that you are dealing with memories now so that you will be free to live when you reach the USA. God speed my friend.
I am now finding it almost impossible to stay with the ongoing pain and abuse I read about. Perhaps even 45 days is too long to document. God help you my Manus friends.

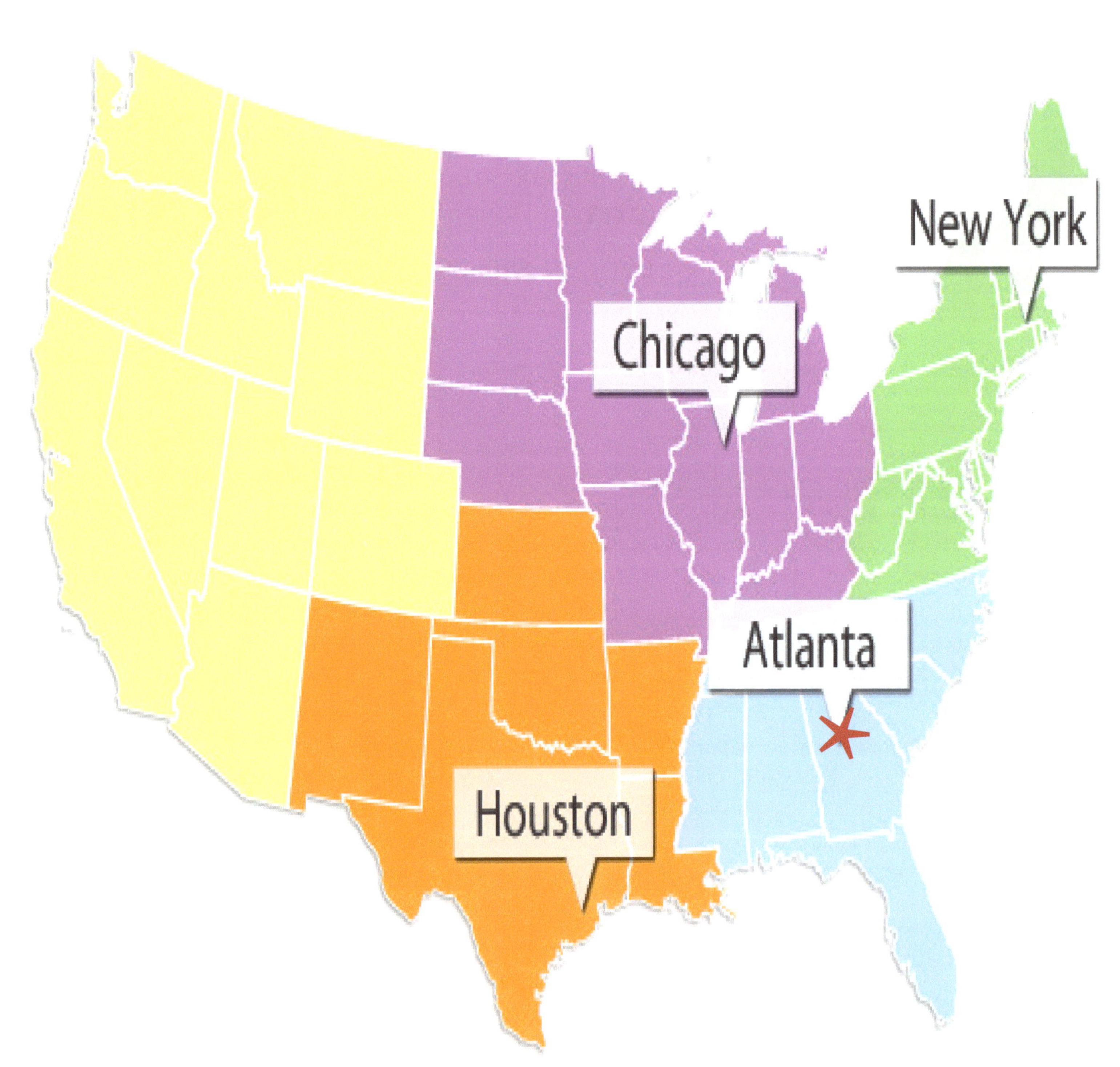

New York
Chicago
Atlanta
Houston

<table>
<tr><td>

13 JAN 2018

</td><td>

"UNHCR Fact Sheet on Situation of Refugees and Asylum-Seekers says neither Papua New Guinea nor Nauru are appropriate places for local integration for the majority of refugees and asylum-seekers, particularly given their acute needs as a result of prolonged detention and harsh conditions". UN Refugee Agency UNHCR

</td></tr>
</table>

MANUS ALERT   **MAN ON MESSENGER**

Security guards have asked asylum seekers to remain in the compounds.

A West Hous resident says the men are worried Asylum seekers say sewage flows past their dining area.

Manus Island: Video purportedly shows sewage flowing down hill near new detention sites
Asylum seekers on Manus Island say local residents have blocked access to their accommodation in a protest over sewerage problems at the site. ABC.

'We are not invisible'
Locals blocked roads to West Haus & Hillside in protest about raw sewage from camps running in gutters. Local people say blockade to continue until problem fixed.

JILL: Morning Man. Hope your classes are good.
MAN: Good morning aunty I'm having my breakfast. Today is final day of class and we will know our destination Today at end of the class.Have a good day.

JILL: How exciting.
MAN: Hi aunty. My state is Georgia State Atlanta city.

JILL: I've been to Atlanta. It is one of our favourite cities.
MAN: Really?? So I'm lucky . Am I ??
JILL: I think so. It has a very multicultural population and is where Martin Luther King spent a lot of his life.
MAN: Yes I heard them when I was in Myanmar CNN news station , Olympic stadium, civil rights.......
JILL: Yes that is the place. I went there to a conference.
MAN: I'm so hoping that we meet again in there.
JILL: We want to contact people from our faith community and ask them to say hi to you when you get there. Can you give me your real name again so I can send it to them as it is hard to scroll back and find it and I simply think of you as Man.
MAN: My real name is Aung Saw Lim.

Wonderful, Man has an actual place to focus on!! This is truly a turning point. I can literally leave the shit on Manus for a while and celebrate Man's escape from hell.

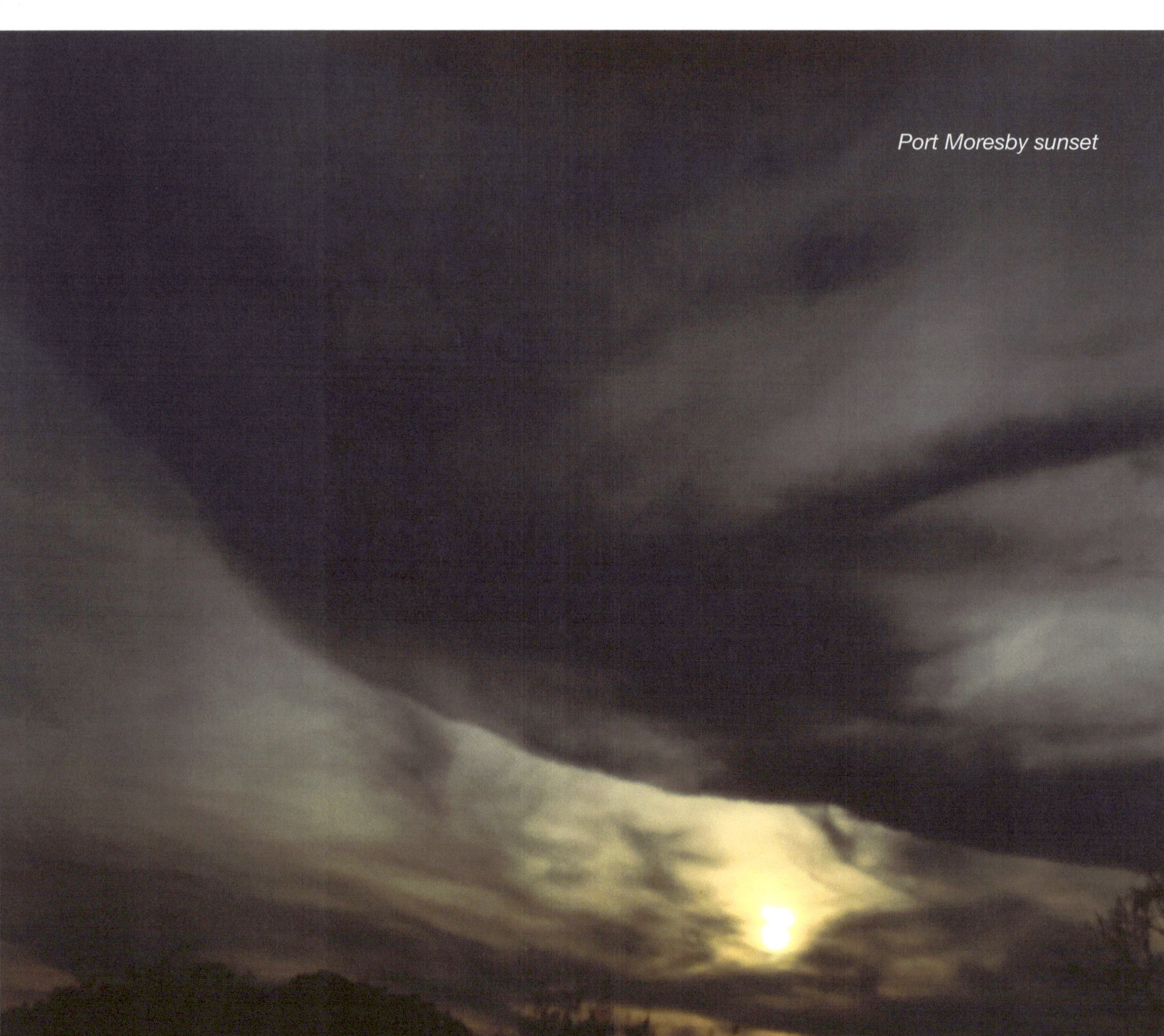
Port Moresby sunset

"Police on Manus Island say they have cleared a roadblock by residents outside new asylum seeker accommodation. ... The protest was the fourth blockade since the forced relocation of men to the detention centre. Neighbouring residents blocked access to the West Haus and Hillside". ABC News

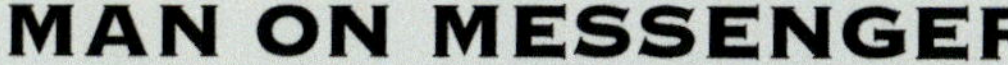

MANUS ALERT

MAN ON MESSENGER

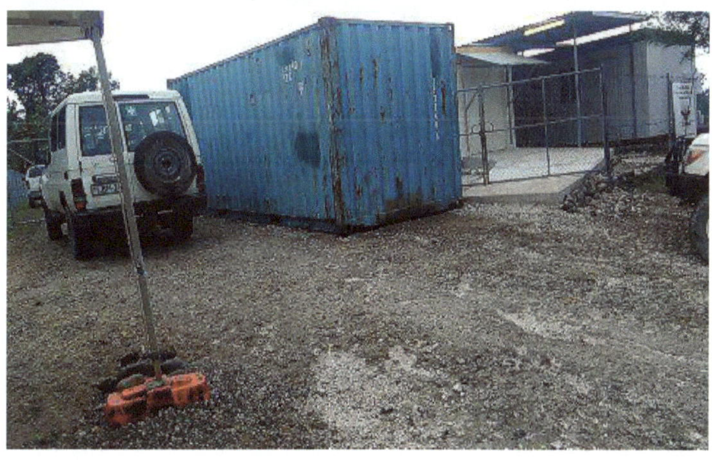

This is IHMS in East camp. Sick men could not go to medical appointments from Hillside or West Haus today as roads are blocked & security told men not to leave camps for safety reasons.

Work started this morning on the smelly and dangerous raw sewerage leaking from West Waste Haus toilet waste tanks.

IHMS = company contracted to run the medical centre.

JILL: OK. Were your classes helpful.

MAN: Yes aunty. We could know a lot of information. Aunty how is Atlanta's weather??

JILL: David says he thinks it is similar to Burma but it can snow. When we were there it was warm and pleasant.

MAN: Now is winter time?

JILL: Type Climate Atlanta into your phone?

MAN: I'll aunty thanks.

JILL: Looks like it has a very wide climate range. Much bigger then here. Is anyone else going to the same place as you?

MAN: I'm not sure aunty...

JILL: Ok

MAN: But I don't really fear about my trip because IOM staff is will be at airports.

JILL: I am sure you will have some initial settlement help.

MAN: Thanks.You are still thinking about me even now I'm leaving PNG..Thank you so much aunty.

JILL: Of course. I will until you forget me.

MAN: Oh please don't say like this it makes me sad. Aunty off to sunset. See you again aunty.

JILL: I still see people here or talk to them on FB 6 years after I last saw them so don't worry.

Man shares his excitement but almost no fear at losing contact until almost the end of the post and then moves away from his feelings quickly when I raise the possible change in our friendship. I remember my reluctance when I left friends in South Africa but know it doesn't help to pontificate. Man needs to learn for himself that there will be many relationships that simply stop but some mature and continue to grow for ever.

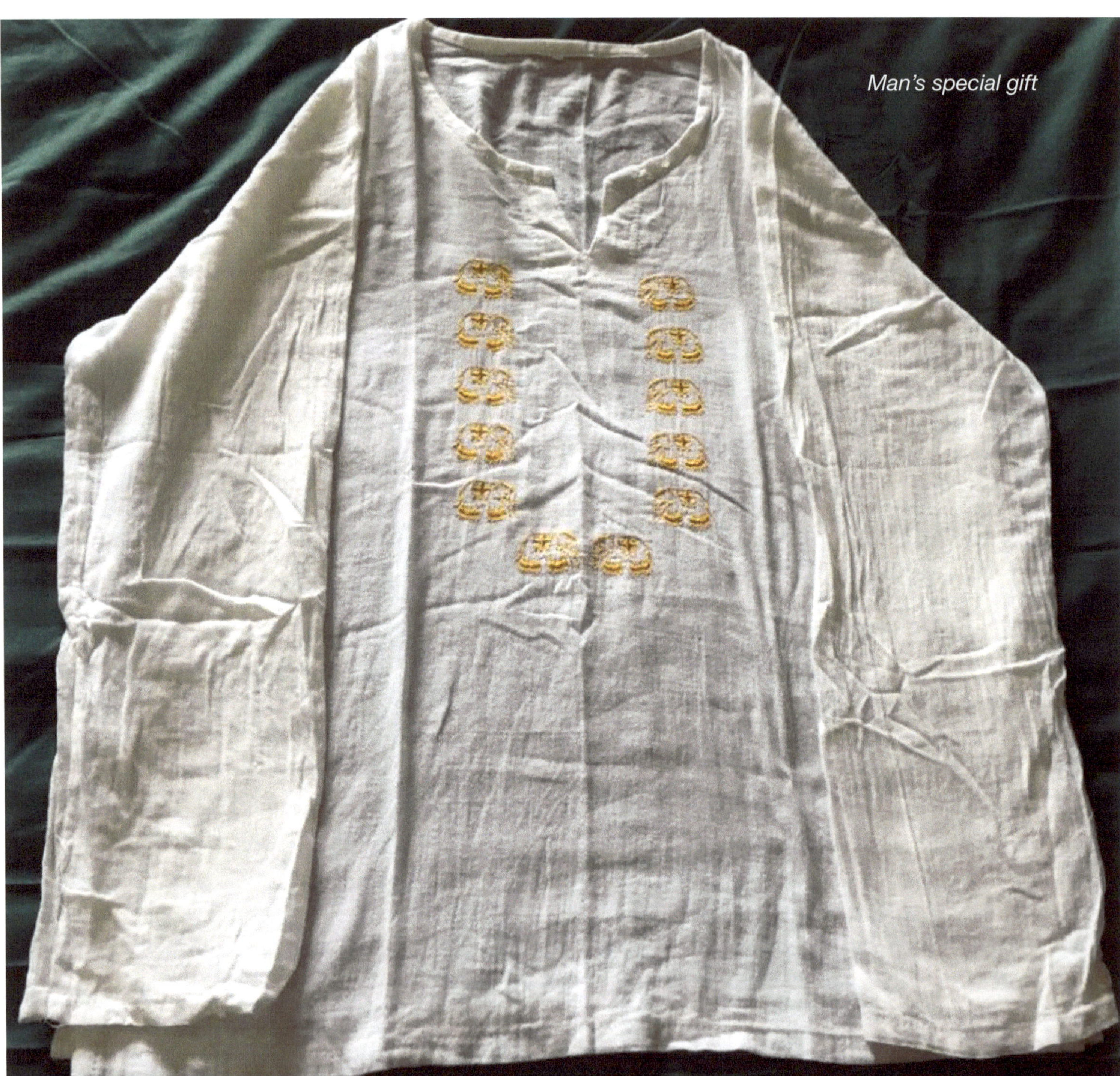

Man's special gift

15 JAN 2018

"Refugees on Papua New Guinea's Manus Island say guards from a security company have seized control of two refugee facilities. Kingfisher is a Manusian company vying for security contracts with Port Moresby's Paladin". Radio New Zealand

MANUS ALERT

MAN ON MESSENGER

They locals are demanding to fix the sewerage system which is causing health issues. It is very close to the Hillside mess where they cook for all the refugees and non-refugees.

The smell is disgusting and will effect everyone's health. They management doesn't care for refugees or even the local children who walk close to the sewerage drain. It's uncovered and smelly all around.

Refugees from West house must walk through the sewerage drain passing to the Hillside mess for their meals. Some carry their food to West Haus camp as the Hillside mess is inadequate space to sit and eat. They have no proper cover for the food when they carry it.

Now the management officials (Australian) are negotiating with the local land owners. The management should have done this sewerage system properly before they brought the refugees and non-refugees. Health care is paramount. We bring you this to your concern. Do not neglect the consequences of this matter.

MAN: I met with a Burmese interpreter in my orientation culture class. I saw him last about four years ago in Manus. He is an interpreter but he is like a mentor. That's why everyone respects him, even Rogingan and Burmese Muslims. Sometime he scolded us if we talked about Negative things too much . I met with him quite of a few time in Choka the isolation zone . He was treated me like a brother, not like interpreter and detainee. Sometime he ate food with me . He said " I don't care even if I lost my job". He was very close with us. According to ABF rule he was not allowed to eats with us. He was also not supposed to speaks without permission from IHMS or security.

He has lived in Australia for above 25 years now. He lived in Shan State in Eastern Myanmar.

The last time we met in Manus we talked about our cultures, foods, religion and traditional clothes. Yesterday he gave me a top in toilet and gave me a top from Cambodia where he went for a holiday.

He said "" I'm always thinking about that top for you how can I give you . I bought it with me at all when I have to come to PNG . I had to took it back to Australia for many times".

I love Man's story. It is wonderful to know that there have been relationships which held Man through the hell he cannot bear to talk about. I knew that Man had been in solitary confinement and believe it was for his own protection but this history he has kept to himself. Thank you so much Man for this gentle love story between a detainee and a guard/interpreter. It revives my belief in humanity. Please treasure and wear his precious gift. Let it comfort you when times ahead are not as easy as you might hope. Wear it also with pride and joy. I know there will be many times to celebrate.

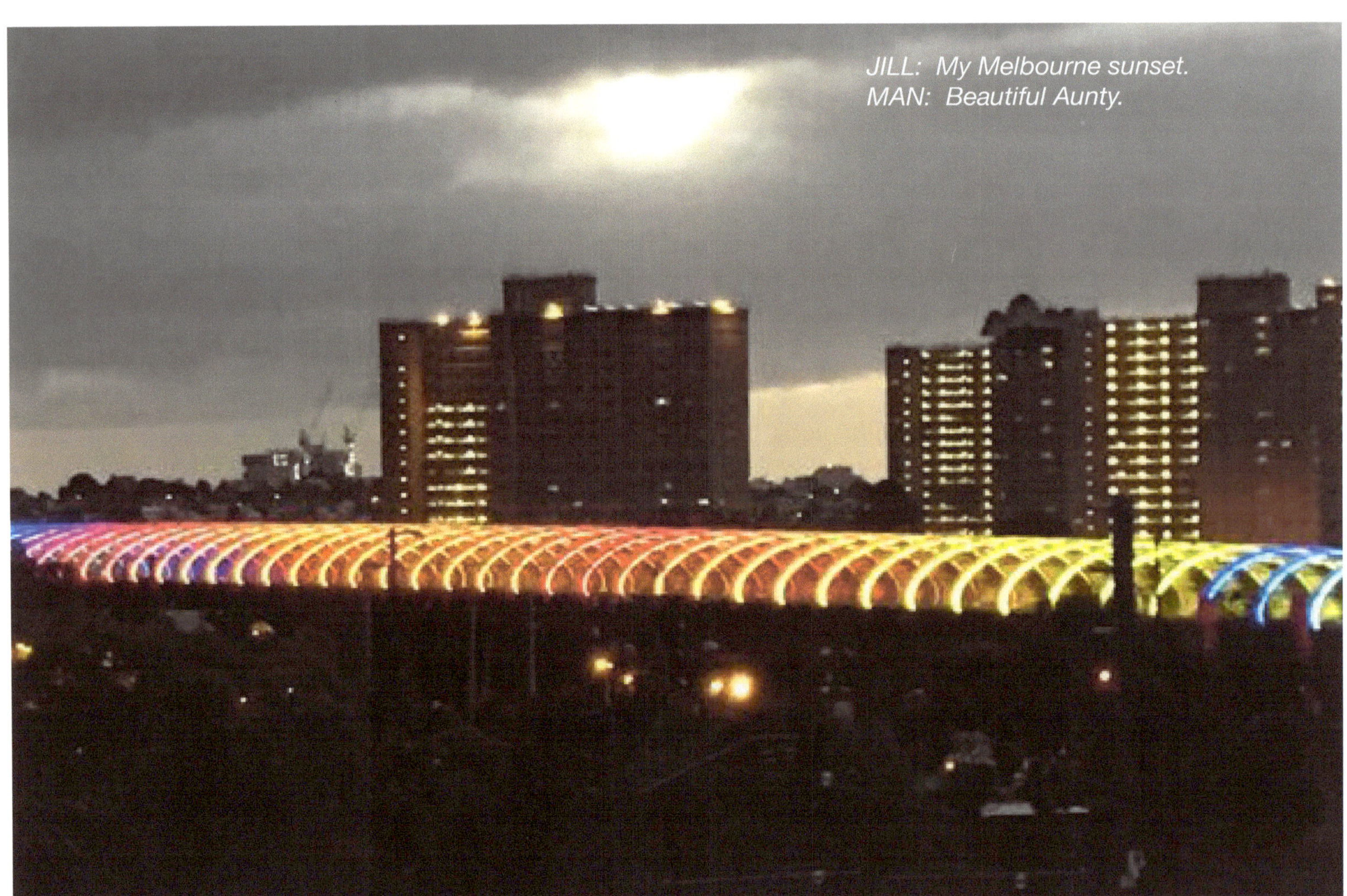

JILL: My Melbourne sunset.
MAN: Beautiful Aunty.

"Kingfisher guards were seen entering the West Haus and Hillside compounds. 'Kingfisher staff came in and sent Paladin officers out,' Iranian refugee and journalist Behrouz Boochani said men from a firm called Kingfisher Security claimed they would be providing security from now on". ABC News

MANUS ALERT   MAN ON MESSENGER

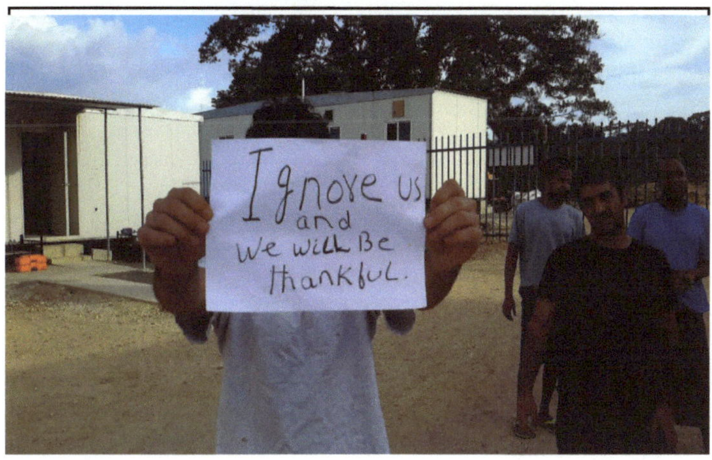

Tuesday
16 January 2018
167th day of peaceful protests
West Waste Haus Manus
Ignore us & we will be thankful
@ManusAlert

MAN: Soon I leave from here . Even you are in Oz and I'm in PNG, my feeling is a bit closer . But US and Oz too far. Very very sad even we hadn't meet each other.

JILL: Me too Man I am sad but so happy that your life will begin again. I believe that one day we will meet. Perhaps in the USA perhaps New Zealand and maybe even at my beach house. I dream of taking you for a walk to see my sunsets over the sea.

MAN: Aunty you know about me a bit . I'm always avoid attachments and responsibilities but I feeling is a bit sad for Manus men.

JILL: Man I have been scared of attachment all my life because of scary childhood so I understand. That does not mean that I don't care about people. It just means I find it hard to let people know. I am very sad for those people who are not leaving Manus and I understand your sadness for them and for yourself. Manus has been a very big and hard part of your life.

MAN: Yes I think that this is good attachment because their life is hopeless at the moment. My attachment is not for individuals it is for all . So my attachment is good.

JILL: Yes Man.

MAN: There are lots of clouds so there will not be a sunset tonight.

Man is amazing. He is able to see his own psychological process and give himself permission to care. I hope this is a beginning that will blossom into many new and wonderful attachments that fill him with joy. I know for myself that I may write less and become occupied elsewhere........ but I will not forget Man or our deep friendship.

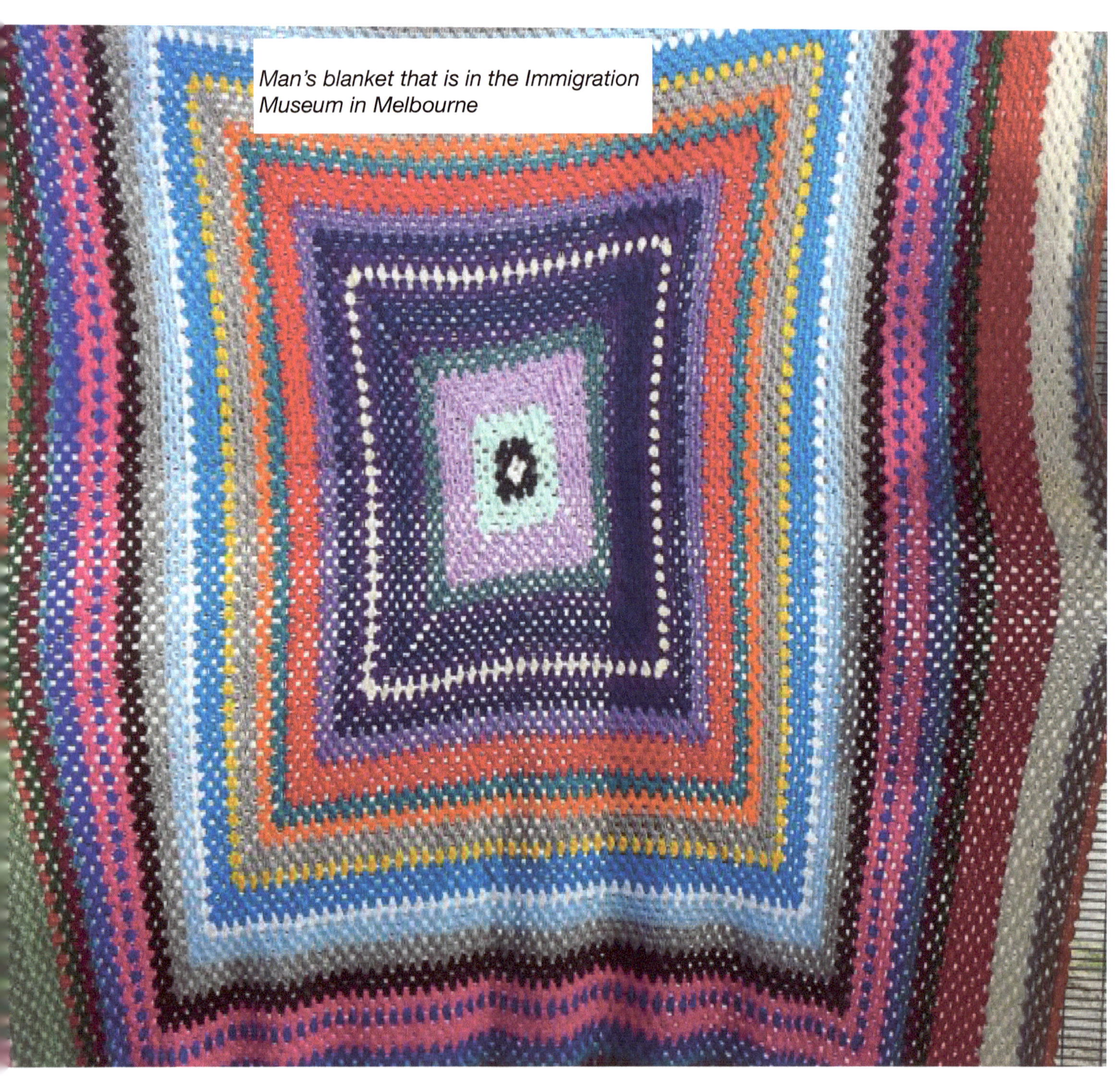
Man's blanket that is in the Immigration
Museum in Melbourne

<table>
<tr><td>

**17
JAN
2018**

</td><td>

"A look inside Manus Island refugees' new home draws criticism. Protests about the treatment of refugees on Manus Island are held in cities across Australia as first footage out of the refugees' new home appears to show unfinished accommodation and no power".
ABC News

</td></tr>
</table>

MANUS ALERT   MAN ON MESSENGER

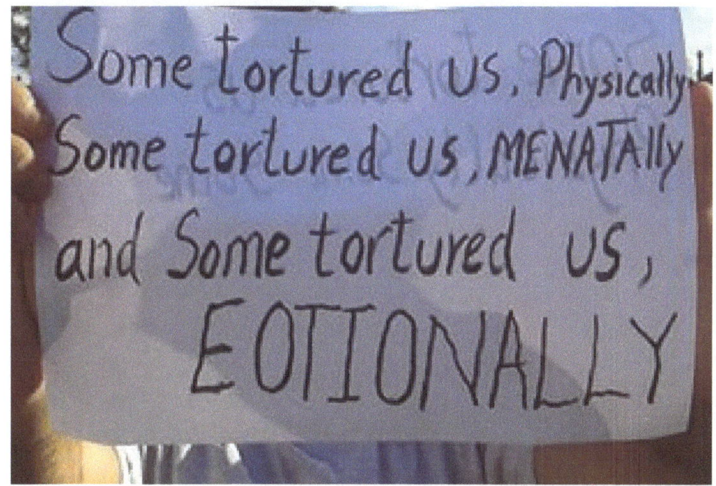

Manus Island security contract dispute leaves asylum seekers feeling 'unsafe' ABC
$580,000 a day.
$22,500 each security guard, each shift.
$1,000 each man guarded, each day.
But Paladin guards couldn't stop local security company kicking them from the camps. Manus is not safe. We are worried.

MAN:: Here is answers for Museum.
My Full Name Is Aung Saw Lim.
I Was Born In Yangon Division- Myanmar
I Grew Up In Yangon Division As Well.
 How did you come to start learning to crochet?
Two Of Australian Case Managers Taught Me Crochet And Knit.Crochet And Knit are Same an Advocator Of Mine.
I Gave My Crafts To My Friends (Australian, New Zelander And Some Detainee).
Were you able to sell any for income?
 I Had have Sell A My Crocheted Blanket For Extra Foods . When I Was In Detention Center.
I Will Always Contact With You All.. Thanks Again For Looking After My Crocheted Stuffs In Museum.
I Crocheted Poppies for World War2 Memorial Day.
WAR Is Very Important Issue for all of us.
Not many detainees are Interesting In craft. Some like to draw.
Jill and I met on Facebook.
We have no choose that's why I will go to US. It is much safer then PNG.
Life Is weird so I have small expectation of US.
I'll crochet In iy future. Crochet, knit and do other handcraft as hobbies and activity.

Man chose not to answer several questions because they were too personal. He does not like talking about his parents or heritage.

I wonder whether I will ever feel comfortable using Man's given name. Perhaps in the future I will remember Aung Saw Lim but "MAN from MANUS" will always stay with me.

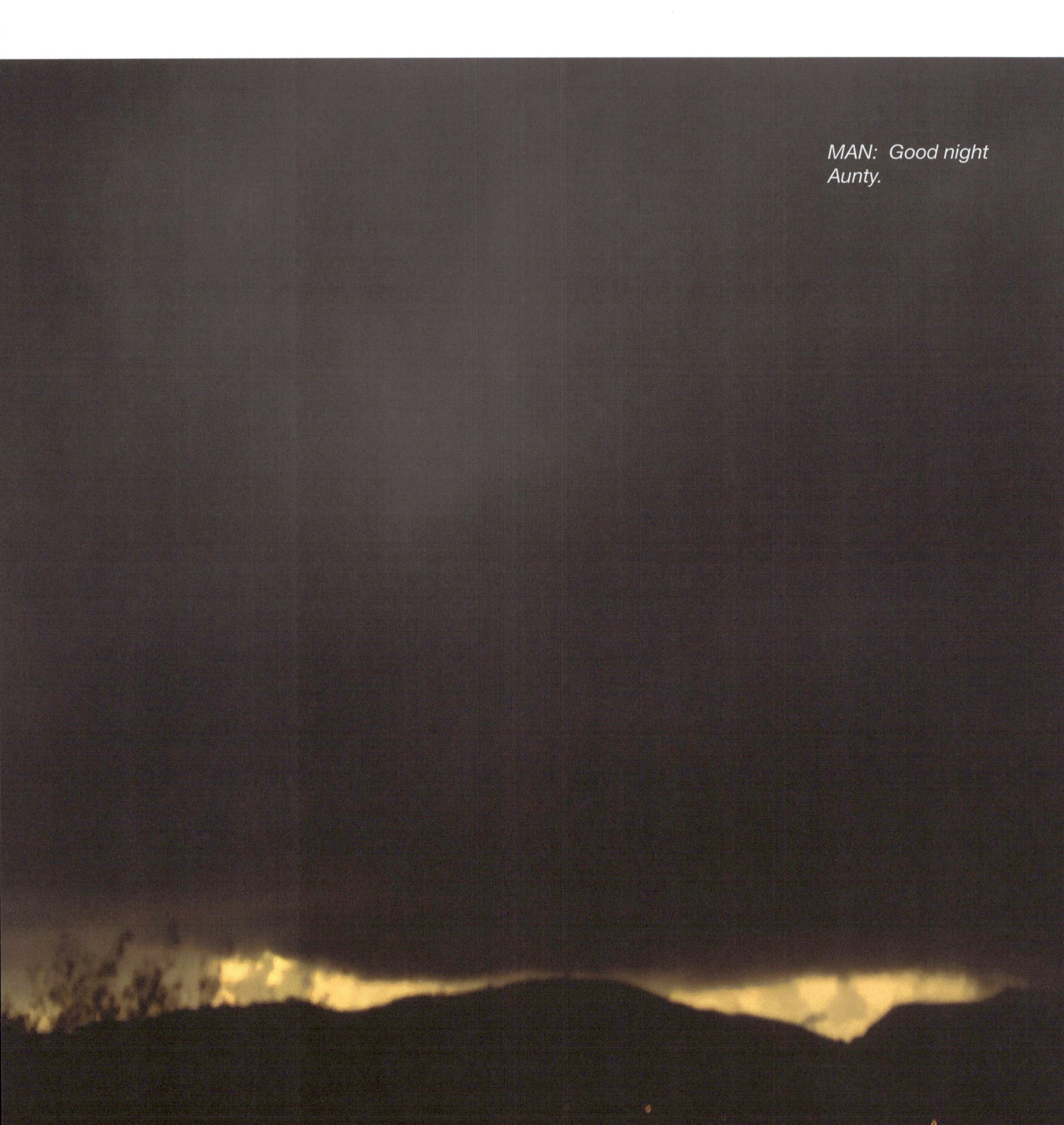
MAN: Good night
Aunty.

"Dutton refuses Senate order to release details of refugee service contracts on Manus. Home affairs minister says disclosing information risks relations with PNG as standoff continues over use of local labour for security contract". Ben Doherty The Guardian

MANUS ALERT   MAN ON MESSENGER

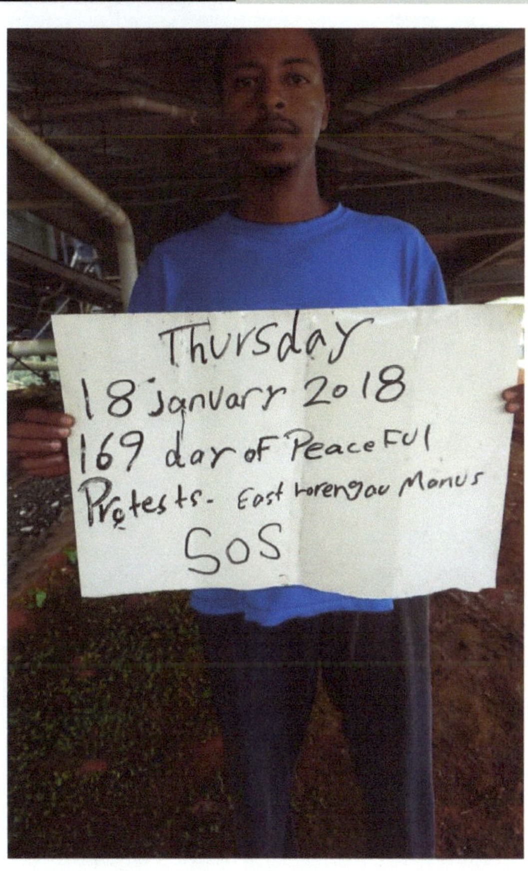

MAN: Aunty how is the first book ?? I don't want that the readers are very bored to read about me.

JILL: It will not be boring to people who want to know about how detention affects people.

MAN: I want you to write about Manus because I feel sadness when I separated from the others. That is what I want to highlight. It is for those left behind. Aunty I can't see a photo because the picture is full of sadness from when I left from Manus.
Abu didn't follow me to bus stop because he was too sad.
LATER

JILL: I heard that very cold in Atlanta now Probably you better knit a jumper quickly.

MAN: I brought two of my jumpers.

JILL: So you will keep warm. Good night Man sleep well.

MAN: You too aunt

I hope I have done Man proud by focusing not only on him but also on his friends and the hardship they face. I know that I have become much more aware of their plight by forcing myself to focus on what they have written in Manus Alert and by looking meticulously through the things that have affected their lives in the last month and a half.
I feel wrung out and traumatised by their journey. Oh how awful it must be to live this never ending Armageddon.

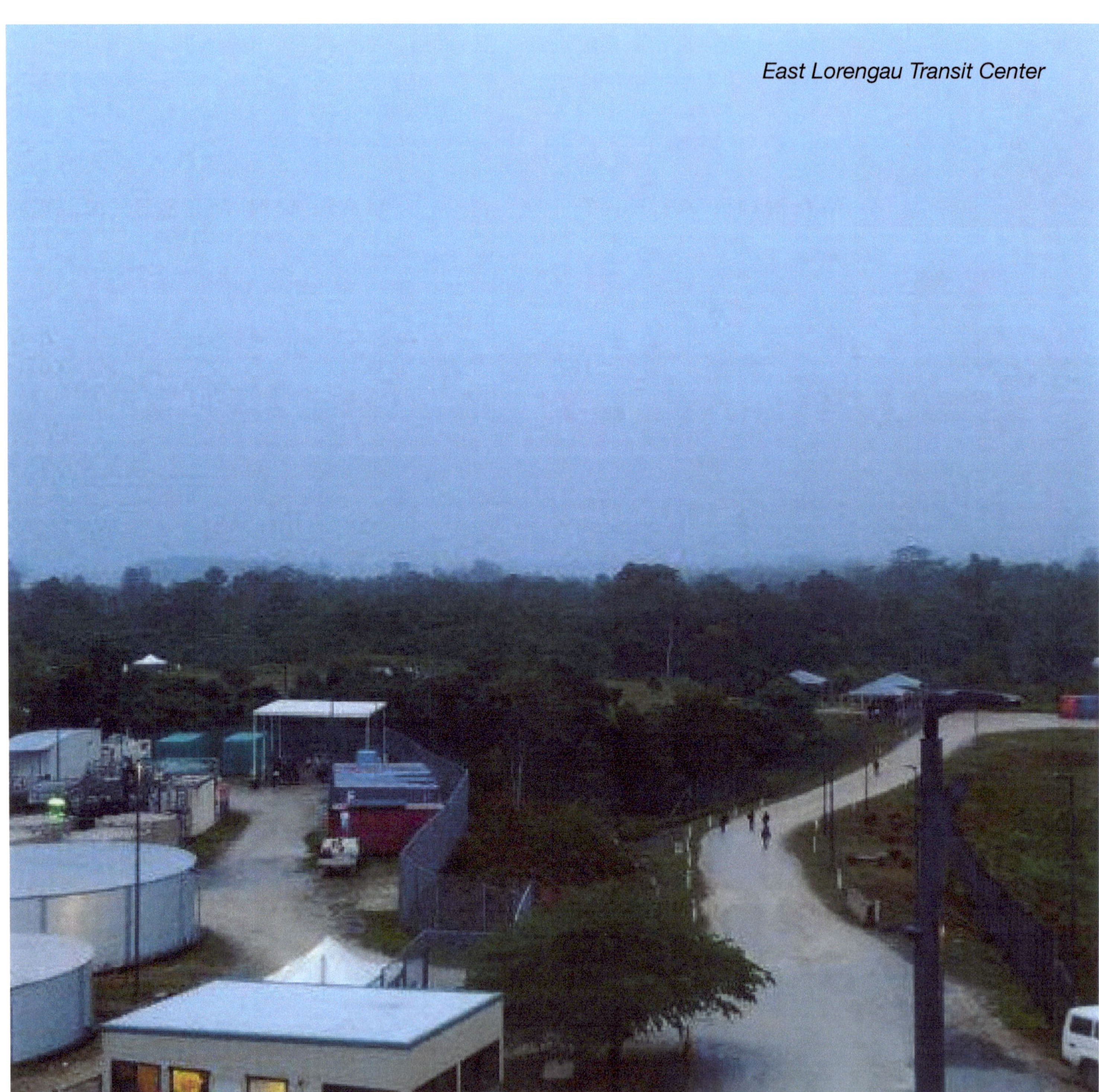
East Lorengau Transit Center

<table>
<tr><td>

**19
JAN
2018**

</td><td>

**"The Minister needs to act urgently to evacuate refugees and asylum seekers off Manus Island so they can get the health care, the security and protection they need. Without urgent intervention, we fear a repeat of suicides like those that rocked #Manus Island last year".
Refugee ActionCollective**

</td></tr>
</table>

MANUS ALERT   MAN ON MESSENGER

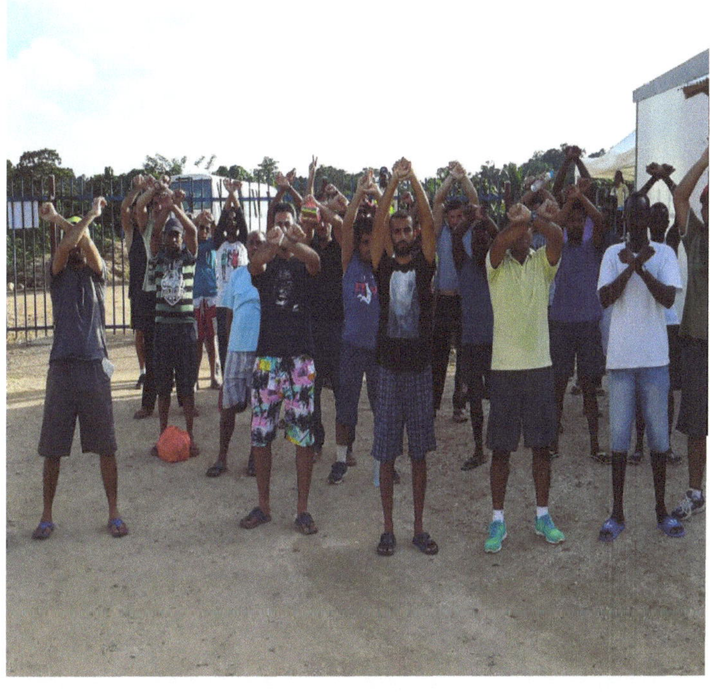

170th day of peaceful protests
West Waste Haus Manus
SOS

MAN: Just recently I chatted with a my Manus friend from East Loremgau Transit Center. He is very depressed about his future after four and half years in the death sentence zone. He wants my advices about how to moves to Pom but he doesn't have medical issues. Unfortunately he can't moves to Pom unless he signs a PNG resettlement agreement but he doesn't want to settle in PNG. He said "I would like to change new place".

I can't get involved with his life. His situations is very sensitive so I said "for myself I would wait in Manus until I fly to US . But I don't know for you". His answers is made me very sad.

"Don't you think staying for more than 4 and half years in Manus is enough for me?"

I did not answer his question. No words to reply. I'm sure that his mind and situations is on very thin string.

He is very interested and excited about my new place. He asked my State and City. This is his message ""When you get there please send me pictures of your happiness".

I am also without words. What does one say to a man trapped in the Manus hell.

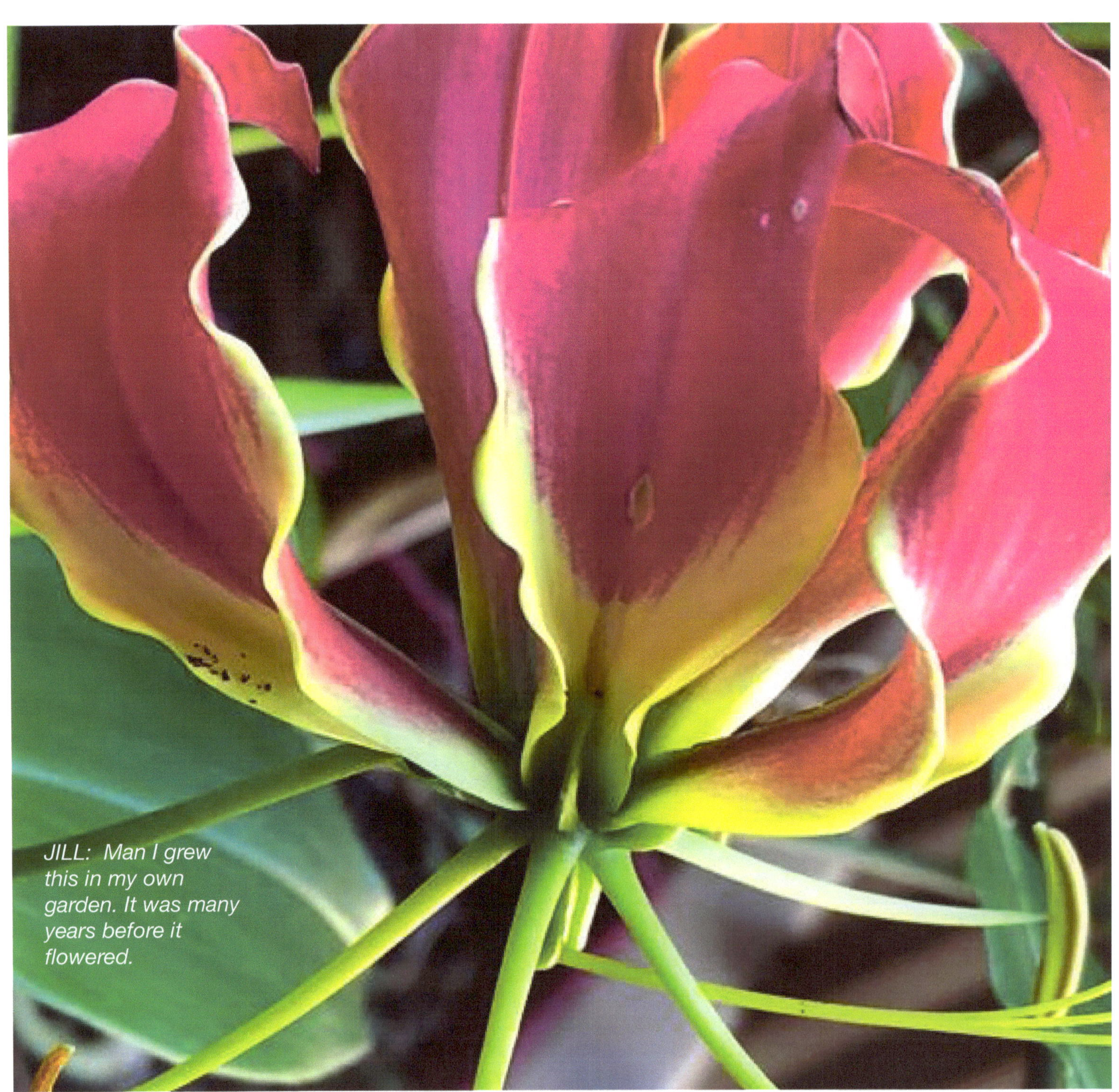
JILL: Man I grew this in my own garden. It was many years before it flowered.

<table>
<tr><td>

20 JAN 2018

</td><td>

"The violent closure of camps on Manus has forced refugees into unfinished facilities with poor access to electricity, food & medical treatment, including torture and trauma counselling".
Asylum Centre Seeker Resource

</td></tr>
</table>

MANUS ALERT   **MAN ON MESSENGER**

A refugee tried three times to kill himself in the last 24 hours in the Lorengau camp. He became unwell with serious mental illness during the last few days. He has been taken to the local hospital but there are no psychological health facilities here or at the hospital to protect him. He is not the only person with mental illness in Manus.

Notice was posted in Lombrum MIRPC on 6 October 2017 that if we moved to Hillside Haus, a canteen would be provided. Many things we were promised were not provided.

JILL: Hi Man I heard from Atlanta friends today they are asking at their meeting this Sunday for someone to meet you and I will let you know as soon as they get back to me after this. Friends are what we call the people who go to my "church" which is not a church but people who meet in silent meditation with God.
MAN: Thanks. Tomorrow and Sunday we have meetings with IOM for our journey so I'll tell you again our flight times aunty
Thanks again.

Food and supplies

You will be provided with three meals a day at Hillside Haus. A canteen will also be provided.

On the left talk of suicide, on the right talk of new beginnings and above, condemnation of a system neither managed nor viable. No words. I am too torn.

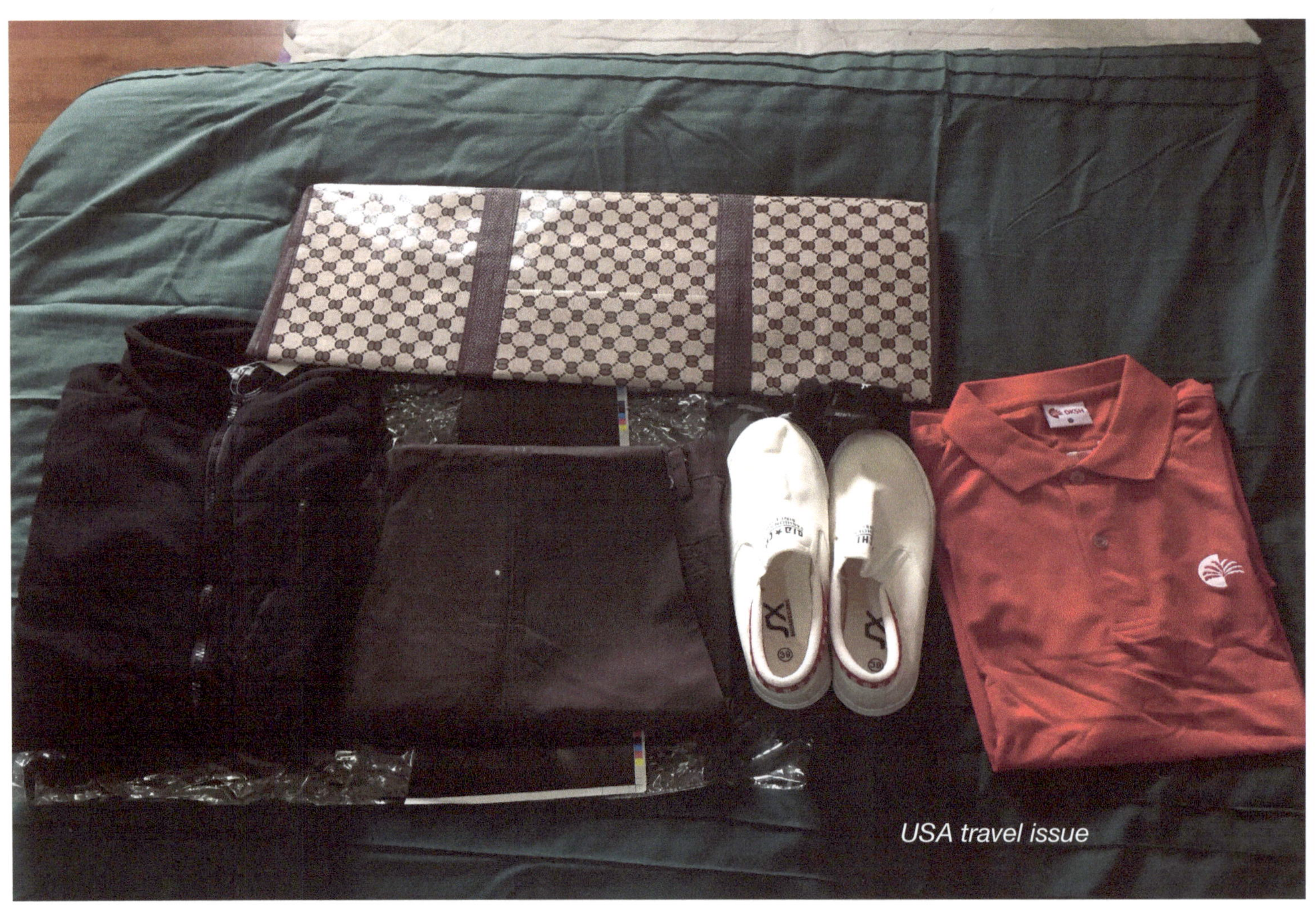

USA travel issue

"The United Nations said the abrupt termination of torture and trauma counselling for the refugees on Manus Island had exposed them to severe psychological harm. Meanwhile, Manus Island refugees are continuing daily protestsagainst their indefinite detention". Radio NZ

MANUS ALERT · MAN ON MESSENGER

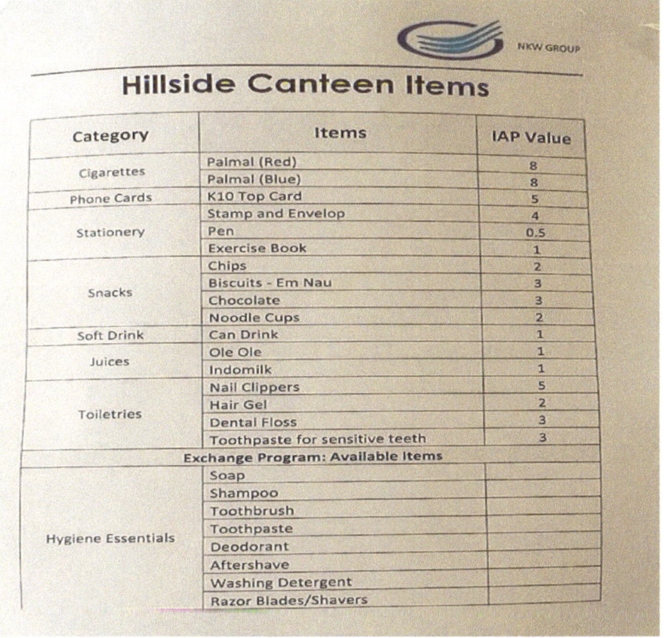

Hillside Canteen Items

NKW GROUP

Category	Items	IAP Value
Cigarettes	Palmal (Red)	8
	Palmal (Blue)	8
Phone Cards	K10 Top Card	5
Stationery	Stamp and Envelop	4
	Pen	0.5
	Exercise Book	1
Snacks	Chips	2
	Biscuits – Em Nau	3
	Chocolate	3
	Noodle Cups	2
Soft Drink	Can Drink	1
Juices	Ole Ole	1
	Indomilk	1
Toiletries	Nail Clippers	5
	Hair Gel	2
	Dental Floss	3
	Toothpaste for sensitive teeth	3
Exchange Program: Available Items		
Hygiene Essentials	Soap	
	Shampoo	
	Toothbrush	
	Toothpaste	
	Deodorant	
	Aftershave	
	Washing Detergent	
	Razor Blades/Shavers	

Hellside Hillside canteen items. 30 points a fortnight, value about Aus $5.80 or $2.90 a week to spend. Exchange Program means take used thing or empty packet to Canteen & get replacement.

MAN: Good morning. Happy Sunday. We are so tired with medication.

JILL: Pleased you have some closed shoes Feeling any better.

MAN: No aunty.

JILL: Sorry.

MAN: Very painful.

JILL: Oh I am sorry. Try to sleep.

MAN: You too.

JILL: I will hold you in the light. Hope that helps.

For so long the Manus men have held their dignity. They protest in silence and respect for each other. Their demands are reasonable but mental and physical wellbeing deteriorates daily. Manus is in chaos and detainees and the local communities who reluctantly host their prisons are close to breaking point.

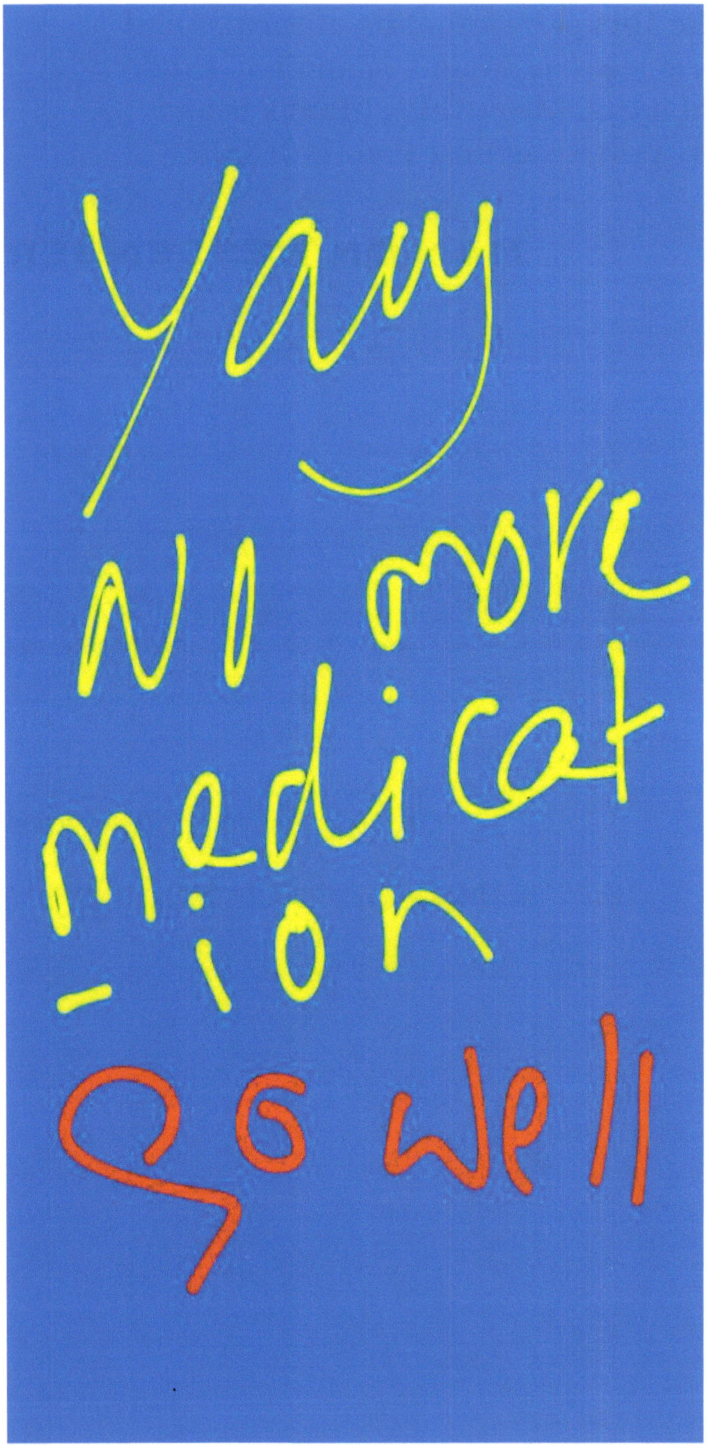

Yay
No more medicat-ion
So well
Done
ROD-62
Bye II
ROD-62

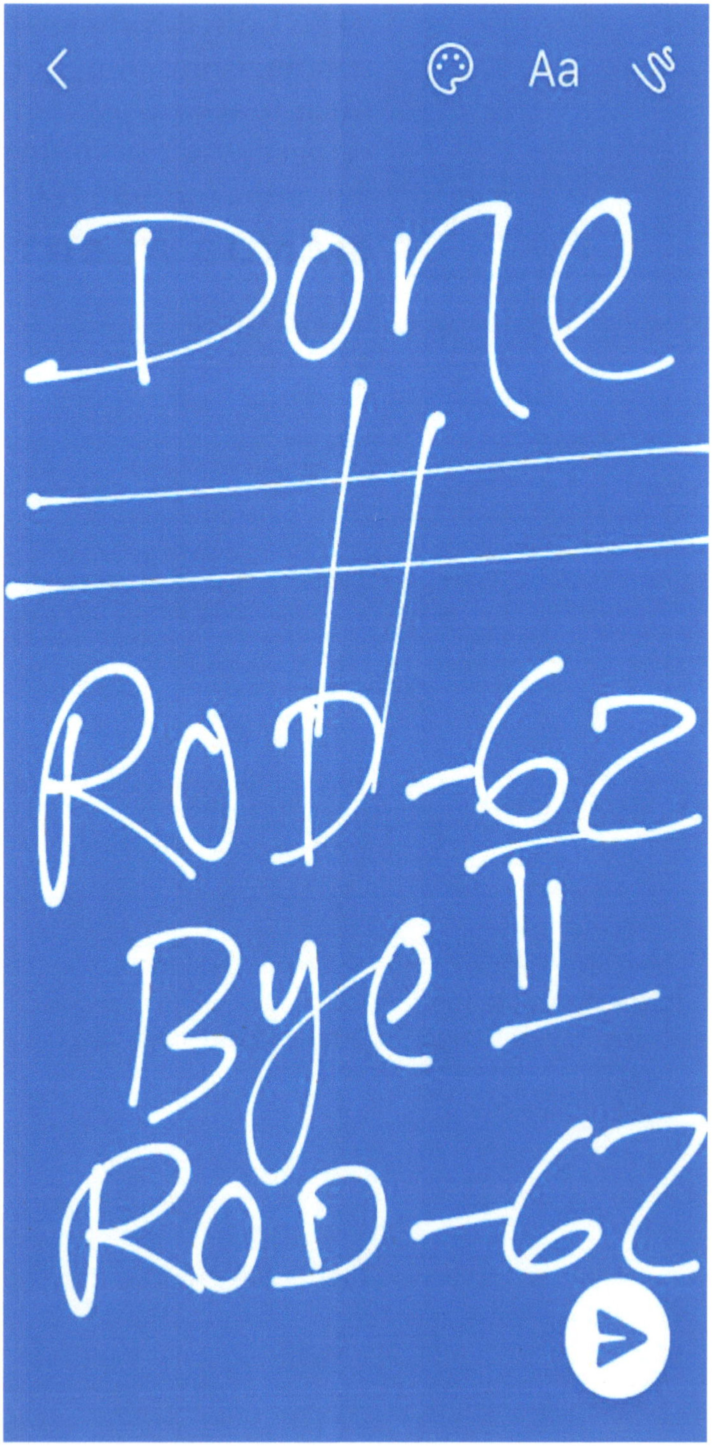

"Men are dying on Manus. Women have been sexually assaulted on Nauru. Children have been so traumatised by offshore detention that they've needed acute psychiatric care in Australia. Families have been ripped apart. It simply can't continue." Daniel Webb, Human Rights Law Centre

MANUS ALERT

MAN ON MESSENGER

Very serious concern regarding cooking pork & eggs in same oil in same fry-pan. We in the Manus HIllside & West Haus Muslim community respect those who want to eat porK but we cannot eat eggs cooked in the same fry-pan & oil as pork. We have raised our concern with the chef. Please show some respect.

This happened this morning:

Me: Chef, good morning. Are you cooking eggs and pork on same fry pan?

Chef: Yes but we clean it.

Me: No you can not.

Chef: Well you should talk to boys who have told us to cook.

Me: It's not my problem who's eating pork. I do respect your beliefs if they are yours. You should respect our beliefs. We want you to use a separate fry-pan ASAP.

Chef: Okay. I'll try my best

Me: Thank you.

MAN: Hi aunty I was too sick n tired with medication. I have never felt like this feeling in my life. I'm a healthy man .But really this medication is makes us extrmely tired.

JILL: Yes because it is killing off all the Maleria still in your system.

MAN: I thought the US government is killing me. I'll go the bed an early tonight. See you tomorrow again. Good night and sweet dreams

JILL: Good night. Hope you feel better in the morning.

MAN: Oh my god I just heard that our flight is Manila to Canada, New York. Is this bad? Anyway I will see Canada airport.

JILL: Yes. Is it tomorrow Man that you go. God be with you and please make contact as soon as you get settled Man.I am missing you already. What time do you actually leave.

MAN: 9.20 am aunty but we must leave from here at 5.30 am.

JILL: Oh wow I have been so busy with people I almost missed your leaving.

Australian leaders have lost the plot. We the Victorian public are continually bombarded with propeganda about Homeland Security, the danger of Sudanese youngsters and our premier's inability to run our state. For this government power, racism and the need to protect Australia from the onslaught of the terrorists from the Islamic hordes trumps all. God save us from Fascism.

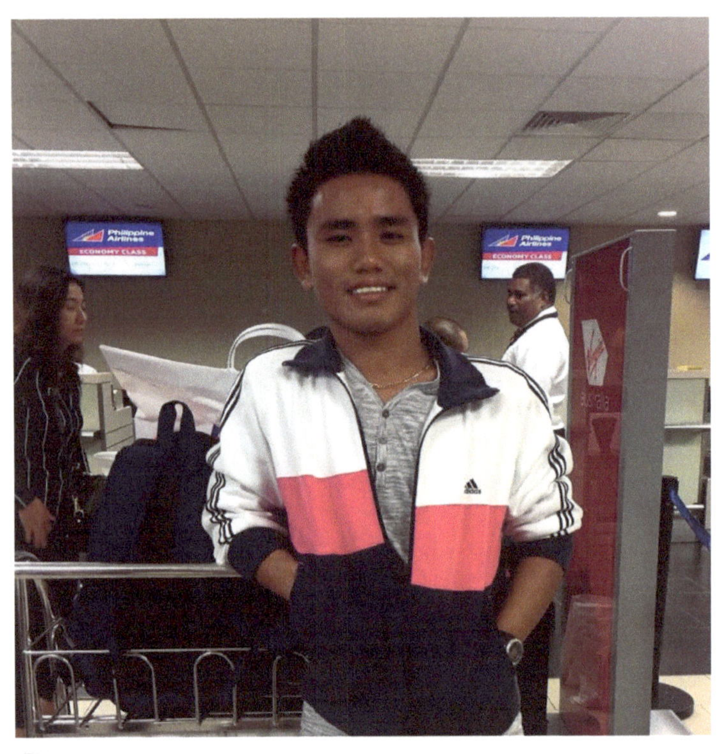

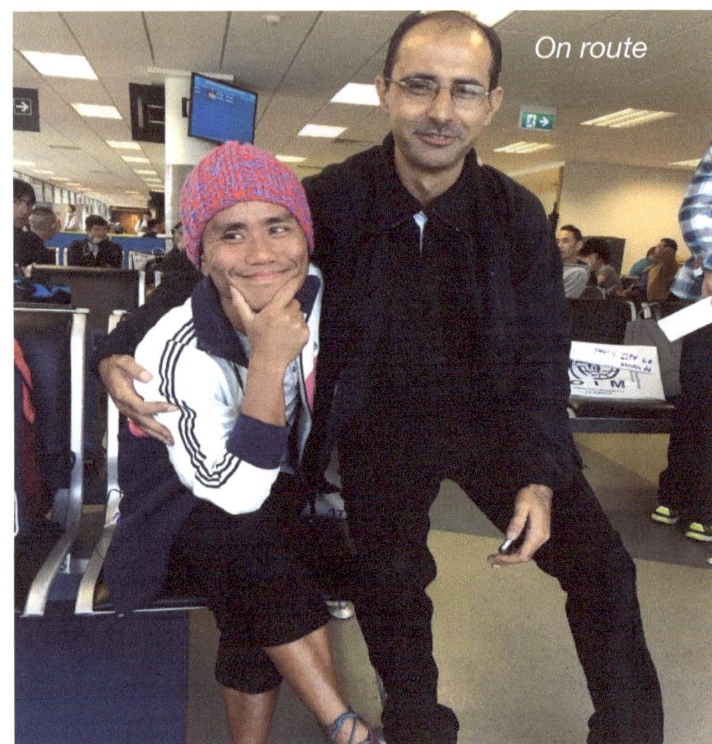
On route

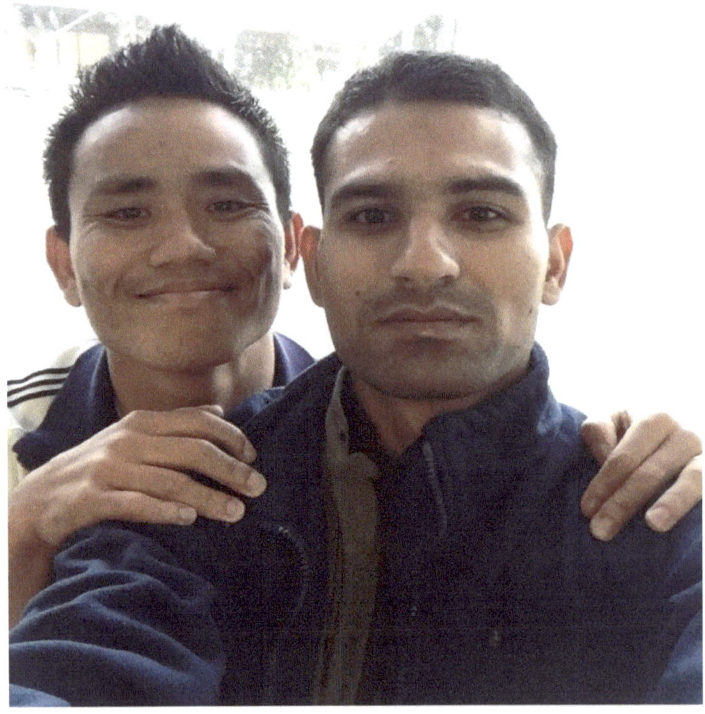

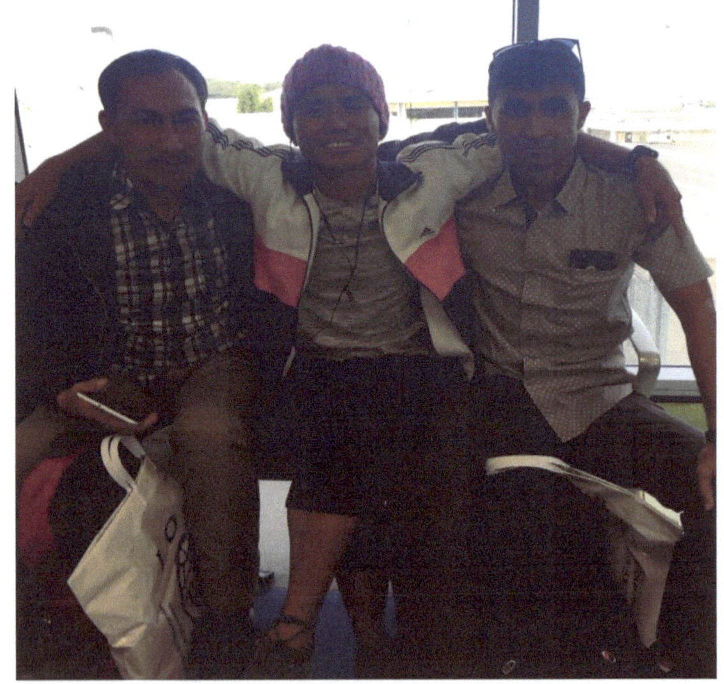

"Second group of Manus refugees departs for US. Fifty-eight refugees left Papua New Guinea for resettlement in the United States on Tuesday as part of an agreement brokered between Obama and Australian Malcolm Turnbull in 2016". The Guardian

MANUS ALERT   MAN ON MESSENGER

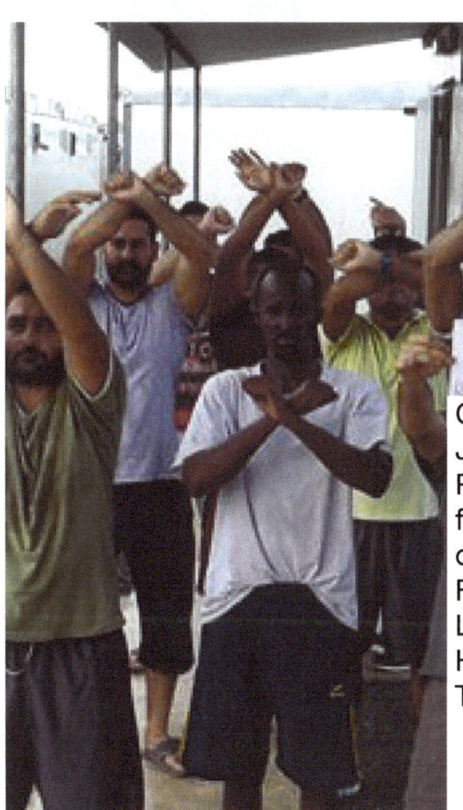

Congratulations
Jacinda Ardern,
PM of NZ,
for the great news
of your pregnancy.
From West & East
Lorengau Manus.
Heavy rain today
Tuesday

JILL: Go well my friend.

MAN: Hi my aunty. Good morning. We are waiting the bus. Happy freedom my friend. It will be a little while before you have. No credit but know I am thinking of you.

MAN: Aunty our flight is Pom to Manila, Manila to Toronto, Toronto to New York, New York to Atlanta

JILL: A long flight. Do you know anybody else who is flying?

MAN: 25 men is until New York . But I'm not sure how many men got Atlanta. Please no worries my aunt I'll be ok.

JILL: I know you will. You are a strong, independent young man.

MAN: Bye see you again. Bus is coming now. Goodbye Australia and PNG. I gave my tears, bloods, time, energies and .... to Australian government. Please keep them as Legacy..Love you all. Thanks my aunt I don't have the parents so I feeling that you, Anne moon (a refugee suporter) and ... same as my mum.

Today: What joy. Man flies out tomorrow hallelujah. Go well Man, my friend and remember lots of pictures.

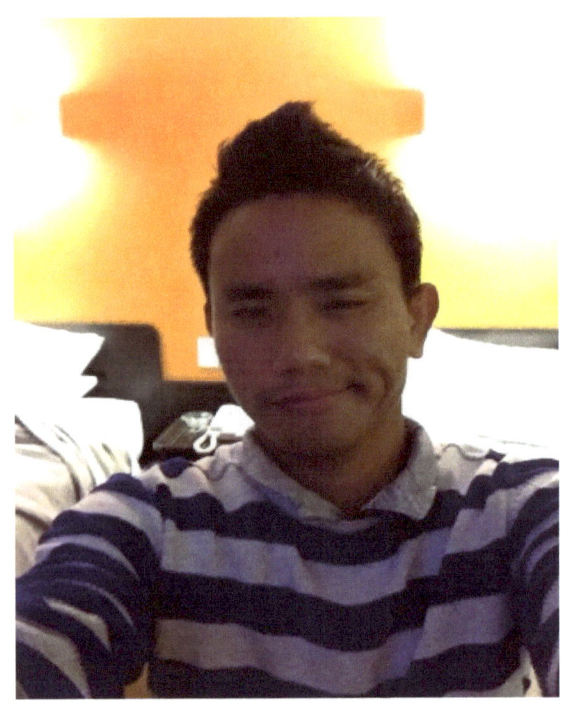

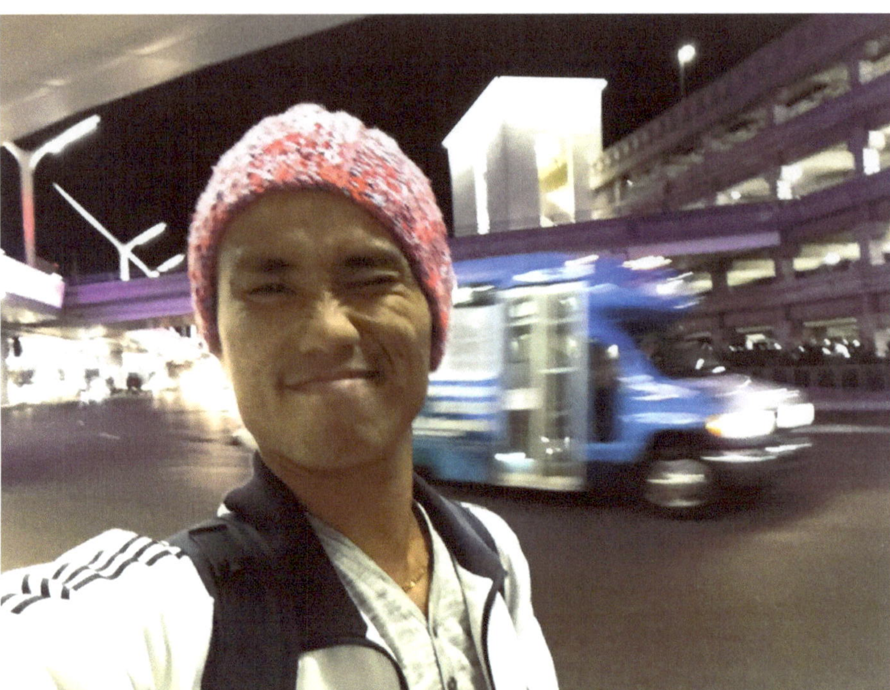

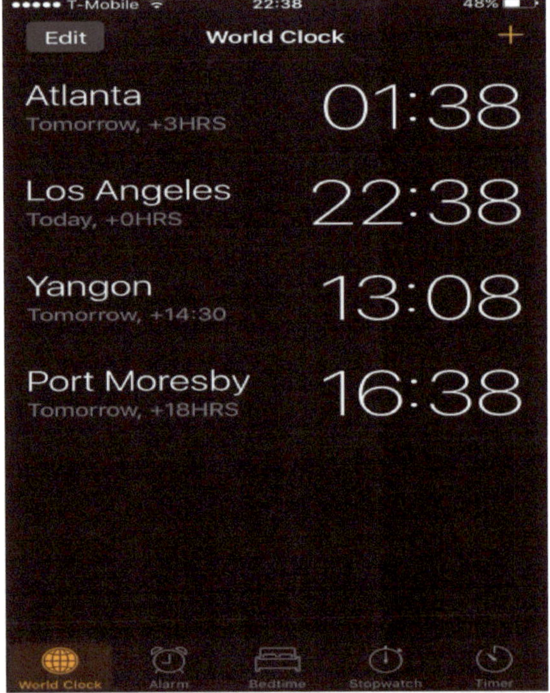

•••• T-Mobile 22:38 48%
Edit World Clock +
Atlanta 01:38
Tomorrow, +3HRS
Los Angeles 22:38
Today, +0HRS
Yangon 13:08
Tomorrow, +14:30
Port Moresby 16:38
Tomorrow, +18HRS
World Clock Alarm Bedtime Stopwatch Timer

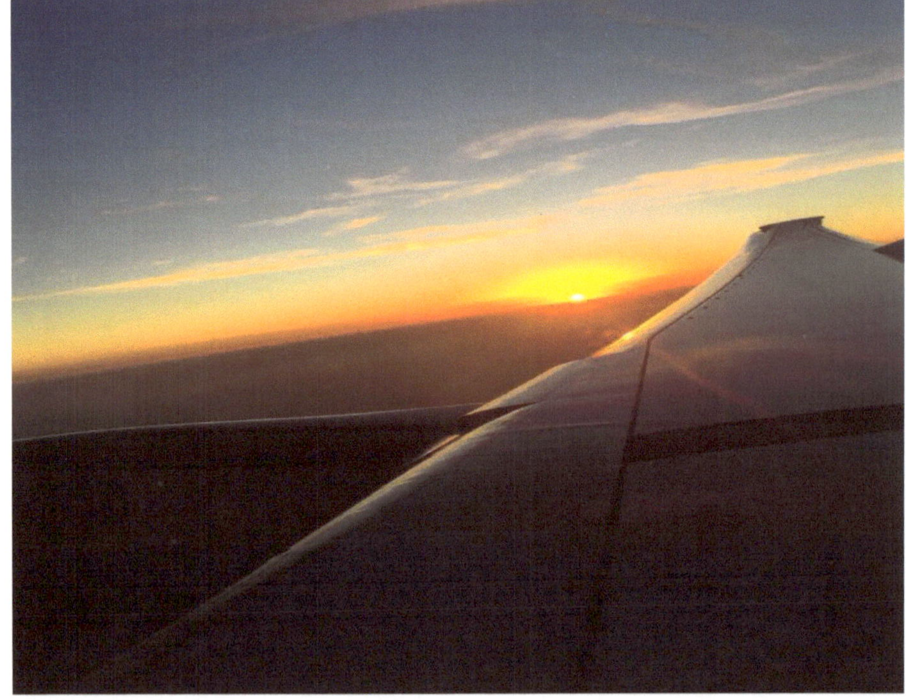

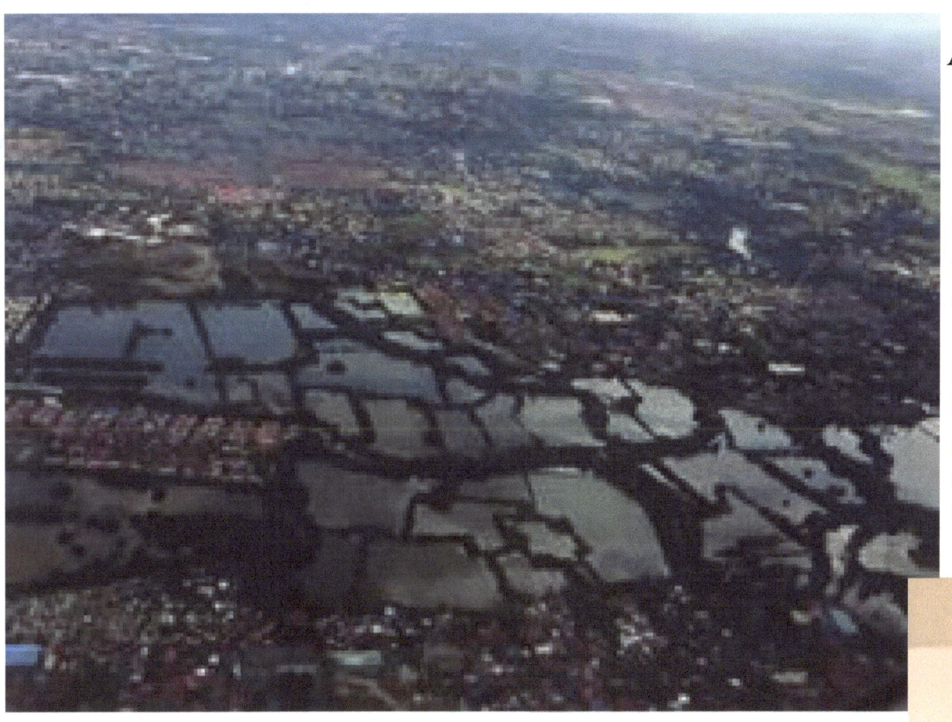

AFTER ARRIVAL IN ATLANTA

MAN: I am no t sure about other guys feeling but i feel that I am a real freed man

When I arrived in Delta Airline's plane and flew out to Atlanta from LA no one esscorted me.

I was busy and confused with the Democratic baggage claim in Atlanta airport but then i caught a couple of trains and I felt nothing scary even though it was my first trip in Atlanta.

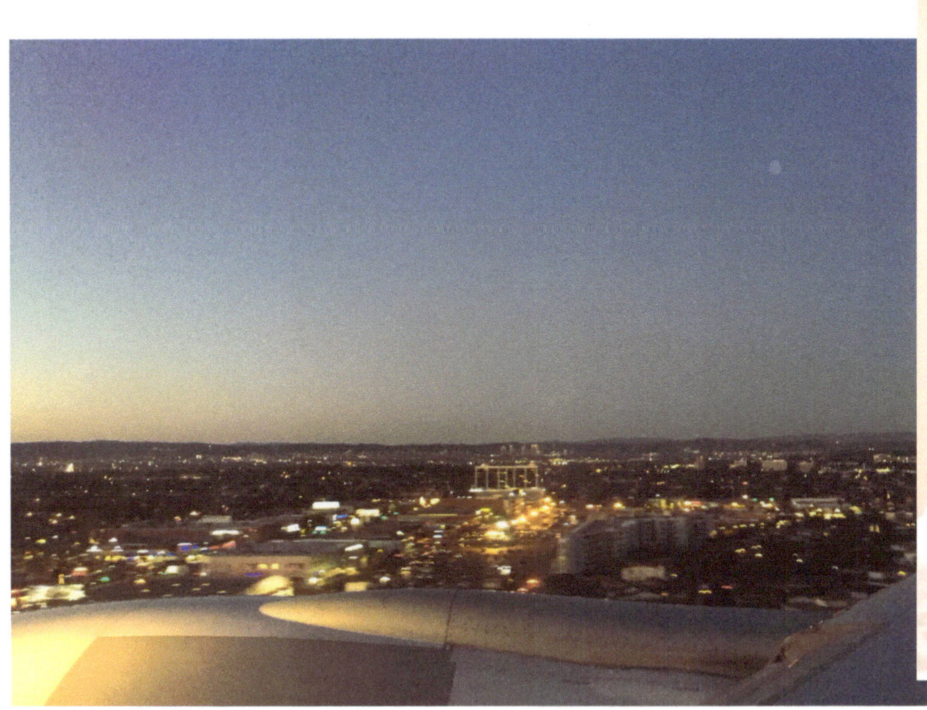

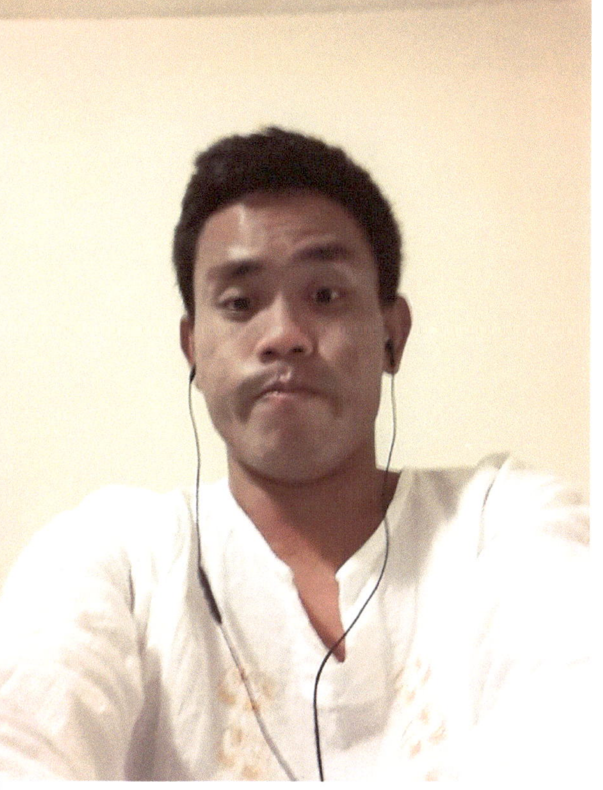

9 781642 557084